AN AVERAGE JOE

JOE HILDEBRAND

ABC Books

The ABC 'Wave' device is a trademark of the
Australian Broadcasting Corporation and is used
under licence by HarperCollins*Publishers* Australia.

First published in Australia in 2013
by HarperCollins*Publishers* Australia Pty Limited
ABN 36 009 913 517
harpercollins.com.au

Copyright © Joe Hildebrand 2013

The right of Joe Hildebrand to be identified as the author
of this work has been asserted by him in accordance with the
Copyright Amendment (Moral Rights) Act 2000.

This work is copyright. Apart from any use as permitted under the
Copyright Act 1968, no part may be reproduced, copied, scanned,
stored in a retrieval system, recorded, or transmitted, in any form
or by any means, without the prior written permission of the publisher.

HarperCollins*Publishers*
Level 13, 201 Elizabeth Street, Sydney, NSW 2000, Australia
Unit D1, 63 Apollo Drive, Albany, Auckland 0632, New Zealand
A 53, Sector 57, Noida, UP, India
77–85 Fulham Palace Road, London W6 8JB, United Kingdom
2 Bloor Street East, 20th floor, Toronto, Ontario M4W 1A8, Canada
10 East 53rd Street, New York NY 10022, USA

National Library of Australia Cataloguing-in-Publication data:

Hildebrand, Joe
  Average Joe / Joe Hildebrand.
  978 0 7333 3190 9 (paperback)
  978 1 7430 9867 7 (ebook)
  Hildebrand, Joe.
  Journalists – Australia – Biography.
  Journalism – Political aspects.
  Australia – Politics and government.
  Australian Broadcasting Corporation.
  070.43092

Cover design and illustration by Hazel Lam, HarperCollins Design Studio
Typeset in Minion Pro by Kirby Jones

Joe Hildebrand is a *Daily Telegraph* columnist and host of the current affairs and lifestyle show *Studio 10*. He also presented the highly acclaimed ABC series *Dumb, Drunk and Racist* and *Shitsville Express*. Prior to this he was a reporter for the *Telegraph*, Australian Associated Press and the UK Press Association. He grew up in Dandenong and went to Dandenong High School before attending Melbourne University, where he did an Arts degree majoring in History and English and co-edited the student newspaper, *Farrago*. He then moved to Sydney, where he still lives. In retrospect he now realises he could have written this memoir in 92 words.

For my mother

Author's note

While I may be a journalist, at least according to some, this book is not a work of journalism. It is not a definitive account of the public events documented herein, nor a history of them. It is a memoir and abides by that philosophy, namely that this is how I remember the things that happened to me. Some of the dates are scarred in my memory, others I have checked and others are vaguely placed. Where conversations are recorded it is how I remember them taking place and the meaning I took away from them. I have certainly recalled them as best I could but others will perhaps contest the exact words spoken, and of course, some names have been changed for legal reasons. In short, I have sought to make this merely an account of my passage through some strange and uncertain times.

Sydney, June 2013

Contents

Australia's Premier Scumbag   1

Secret Origins
Fire and Wood   11
Peace and War   16
The Second Son   27
The True Believers   31
My Grandmother the Drug Dealer   38
The Wide Brown Land   47
Fighting Fires   52
The System   56
Saving Superman   62
A Good Girl   70
The Gentle Art of Dentistry   74
The Little Engine That Could   80
It's Only Words   86
When I See You Smile   89
The Legend of Jason Stan   94
Juliet   102
The Heartbreak Kid   111

The People's Hero
Universe City	119
Big Red	127
Palmerston Street	130
The Hell Train	137
Children of the Revolution	141
The Apprentice	147
Absolute Power	154
The Three-Week Plan	158
Walking the Talk	163
The Revolution Cometh	170
Psycho Journo	178
Cardigan Street	185
Being Specific	191
Rock Star Syndrome	194
The First Cut is the Deepest	199
The Fish	205
The Last Time	211
A Farewell to Arts	214
The Test	220

The Yellow Sun
The Faded Emerald	227
Nice Guys Finish First	229
The Dumb Question	235
The Bear Pit	240
Picking Winners	246
The Knowledge	249
Breaking News	255
Multiplexity	261
Splash	267

Truth and Reconciliation	270
A Fork in the Road	274
Rudd the Great and Terrible	278
Rudd the Campaigner	283
Purgatory	289
The Long Walk Home	291
Arrival	296
Acknowledgements	301

An Average Joe

Australia's Premier Scumbag

Rural Queensland is not a surprising place to find a right-wing minority-hating redneck, however it is a surprising place to find out you are one. In the small town of Allora – which the locals fiercely pronounce *Al*-ora, not Al-*ora*, lest anyone think it might be of ethnic origin – the sun shines warmly on the Darling Downs, injecting the landscape with an unearthly vivid green. And at the Allora Show the grass was positively emerald as I wandered around questioning cattlemen on the merits of a good steer and extracting baking secrets from the Country Women's Association.

I was on the road filming the ABC show *Dumb, Drunk and Racist*, my first attempt at presenting a television series. The premise was that we would take four people from India who thought Australians were, as the title subtly suggested, dumb, drunk and racist. We would then attempt to prove them wrong while at the same time introducing them to as many dumb, drunk and racist people as we could find. It was, to say the least, a somewhat paradoxical ambition. At the end of four straight weeks of shooting I was supposed to gather them all together and ask eagerly, 'So, do you *still* think Australians are dumb, drunk and racist?' to which they would no doubt respond, 'Well, *duh!*'

But the complex narrative arc of highbrow reality television was the least of my worries. Earlier that morning I had woken to the sun streaming through my hotel window and the news that I was Australia's premier scumbag. I would like to say that I am of course speaking figuratively, however in at least one case 'Australia's premier scumbag' was the exact phrase used to describe me – and that was one of the kinder remarks.

The furore had started, as furores always did in the first half of the second decade of the 21st century, on Twitter. Naturally, being a profound, witty and self-effacing sort of gentleman, I was enormously popular on social media. Yet upon checking in to see what latest paeans of praise were there to greet me that day I was alarmed to discover that some people were actually criticising me. Had the world gone mad?

To be honest this was not entirely a new phenomenon. For some time I had known I had an uncanny ability to attract abuse from both the left and the right for precisely the same comment.

In part this was perhaps because I was the only person who worked for the ABC while at the same time working for *The Daily Telegraph*, which was regarded by ABC viewers as an extremely biased right-wing media outlet. Fortunately this view was balanced out by *Telegraph* readers, who regarded the ABC as an extremely biased left-wing media outlet. In fact neither perception is entirely true – which, incidentally, is precisely the sort of comment that would get me in so much trouble.

However, this time the charge was new and unexpected. This time I 'hated disabled people'.

The proof of this heinous crime was a tweet composed at Sydney Airport while waiting for one of that institution's spitefully overpriced coffees. Having an inordinate amount of time on my hands, the cause of which we shall soon see, I had mused on the absurd ordeal one must go through there in order to get a caffeinated drink – which is of course a vital necessity to surviving the absurd ordeal of Sydney Airport itself.

First, you must present at the ordering counter. This in itself takes a staggering amount of time as either A) a pair of Americans in front of you have an existential crisis over why the Latte Grande costs extra with caramel syrup; or B) you wait alone at the counter while the cashier, having mastered the art of self-hypnosis, enters into a staring competition with the toaster.

Eventually the cashier takes your order for the coffee and you go to hand over the money, wondering if a twenty will be enough to cover it. But this of course is premature. First the attendant must ask you for your name and enter it into the register, as though you were checking in for a flat white. 'It's Joe,' you say, and they dutifully nod and type in J-O.

That accomplished, the cashier charges you $6.50 and prints two copies of the receipt, one of which is given to you and the other of which is passed down towards the end of the counter to a barista who, invariably, is not there.

Then, with the sale processed and the docket transferred to someone else's business unit, the cashier resumes staring at appliances. This at least explains the unusually diligent recording of names. By the time the barista has returned from whatever recess of the departure lounge he has been seeking refuge in and fills the requisite number of cups with coffee and milk in a cup for yourself and however many people before you who have long since disappeared to catch their planes, it is entirely reasonable that the entire staff have not only forgotten what you look like but that you ever existed in the first place.

This is why, while the lines for almost everything else at an airport – check-in, security clearance, flight boarding – are as long and winding as the Yellow Brick Road, queues at airport cafés are rarely more than a handful of people. For purposes of travel and national security it is imperative that both the passenger and the staff member perform their respective duties or the airport would cease to function. However the café has no such raison d'être – it is merely a contest of wills, desperation versus ambivalence. The result is essentially a war of attrition in which only the laziest and most decaffeinated are left standing.

Should anyone consider this assessment somewhat extreme, allow me to share a story my sister told me. Annie was the sole passenger in an airport lounge and approached the person at the coffee counter, who was the sole employee in the lounge. Indeed, for all either of them knew, they were the only two people on Earth.

After placing her order and offering a clearly denominated bill of legal tender to pay for it, she was, as per protocol, detained by the cashier with a hand gesture. 'Name?' the cashier asked. Having glanced around to confirm that there were no other people in sight, my sister replied both politely and honestly: 'Annie.'

The cashier dutifully nodded, processed the information via the cash register, and printed out two copies of the docket.

The first he passed down the counter to the coffee machine, at which, also as per protocol, no one was in attendance, and then returned to give the second copy to my sister as proof of purchase – all, once more, in accordance with proper procedure. It was then that things started to get interesting. In a breakthrough for productivity, he went back to the other end of the counter, picked up the original order, and proceeded to make the coffee himself. Having completed this task a mere ten minutes later, he placed the coffee on the counter and stared at the receipt while my sister stood in her original position some two metres away.

Still the confused console operator and coffee maker looked searchingly around the empty banks of chairs in the gate lounge like an oscillating fan.

'Annie?' he called out.

This minor episode of life came to mind as I quietly aged at my own coffee counter trying to ignore the sound of my boarding call. Fiddling with my phone for want of anything better to do I opened up my Twitter account. Somewhat aimlessly I typed: 'I just want to say I think it's great that Sydney Airport is providing jobs for the mentally handicapped.'

These words, it is fair to say, were not received with the same casualness with which they were written.

The initial, mild – and what fellow disabled-people-hating people might describe as obvious – response was a few sympathetic retweets and replies that yes indeed Sydney Airport was quite a stupid and frustrating place.

But somewhere in the next 24 hours a young disability activist had come across my tweet and declared that far from being an observation about the airport's various inefficiencies it was in fact a savage attack on the plight of the intellectually disabled. Not only had I maliciously abused an oppressed minority, I had not even used their linguistically correct categorisaton – something which, incidentally, I am yet to see an intellectually disabled person get particularly outraged about.

Ironically, the little thought that I had put into the comment was to use the term 'mentally handicapped' quite deliberately. Like anyone else who had been to high school in the last twenty years I was well aware it was an archaic expression that the academic arbiters of such things had ruled inexcusable. I thus reasoned the use of such a quaint and outdated term would make it obvious to even the most dense or sensitive souls that the comment was a pisstake not just of idiotic airport retailers but haughty and self-righteous jetsetters. I imagined it would be the sort of thing Prince Philip might say. What, therefore, could possibly go wrong?

But of course jokes, once you have to explain them, are no longer funny – as Eddie McGuire and I have since learned. And that rule was proven once again when the activist in question, a no doubt well-intentioned blogger called Stella Young, wrote an article explaining in forensic detail why my remark was so deeply offensive.[1] I still haven't read the piece in question so can't vouch for the merits of her argument but as a newspaper editor I was certainly impressed with her quick turnaround time.

Having no desire to go to war with the disability sector I decided the best course of action was to disarm the

---

1 Offensive to disabled people, I should clarify, not Sydney Airport employees.

situation with my usual infallible charm, and so in the face of the avalanche of abuse now being piled on top of me, I posted the following response: 'I am very sorry for using the term "mentally handicapped". That was really retarded of me.'

For some strange reason this only seemed to make matters worse.

It says something about the level of esteem with which I am held in the community that even calling myself retarded was considered an insult to retarded people. It wasn't long before the level of outrage had reached epidemic proportions, to the point where distant family members whom I wasn't aware had even discovered the internet were inquiring as to whether I was still alive.

Both questions seemed soon to be resolved on national television when an ABC News 24 host asked me to come on his show and debate Stella on the issue. The topic was to be something along the lines of 'Does Joe Hildebrand hate disabled people?' which I felt sure could only reflect positively upon me.

But of course the great immovable laws of geography got in the way. From my small sun-drenched room in Allora I had to reluctantly inform the nice ABC anchorman that as I was in the middle of country Queensland filming a show for his own network, I would unfortunately be unable to make it. The tabloid reporter in me saw the headline from as many miles away: 'JOE HILDEBRAND DOESN'T DENY HATING DISABLED PEOPLE'.

And even this was not to mention the far greater crime in my mother's eyes: 'JOE HILDEBRAND REFERS TO HIMSELF IN THE THIRD PERSON'.

And yet, as I was lamenting this missed opportunity to my best friend back in Melbourne, he suggested that I had in fact dodged a bullet in avoiding a head-to-head confrontation on national television with a young woman in a wheelchair. It was, to put it in public relations parlance, not good optics.

'What are you talking about?' I said. 'I could've smashed the little bitch.'

There was a pause.

'Er, that was a joke,' I reassured him. Ever since he'd become a quadriplegic he'd developed an annoying capacity to become suddenly earnest.

'Yeah, I know,' he said at length. 'It's just that sometimes I worry about you.'

'Oh, come on,' I said. 'It's me. It would've been fine. Everyone knows I'm a nice guy.'

There was another pause.

'Oh, Joe,' he said. 'You really have no idea, do you?'

Where, I wondered, had it all gone so wrong …

PART I

Secret Origins

Fire and Wood

My mother was an excruciatingly shy middle child of two bog-poor Irish Catholics. Her father Jack had in fact had the opportunity to be magnificently rich but, in keeping with longstanding family tradition, had managed to carefully calibrate his financial decisions so as to deprive himself of any prosperity whatsoever.

Jack had grown up on a farm southeast of Melbourne under the whisky breath and horsewhip of a cruel and alcoholic father. The alcoholism he inherited but the cruelty he did not. When the father died and left the farm to Jack and his older brother, Phoncie – an improbable derivation of Michael Alphonsus Broderick – the two young men elected to sell the place at once. It contained no good memories for them. Their sister, meanwhile, decided to become a nun only to later drown in mysterious circumstances. The family's path to happiness seemed assured.

Phoncie, a miserly man whose only two enthusiasms were the card game 500 and observational racism, pocketed his half of the money and put it in a bank account. There it sat never to be touched again until, having died childless and a virgin at 86 years old, he bequeathed his entire estate to the Catholic Church.

Jack, however, had other ideas.

Even in the far outer backwaters of Melbourne the middle of the 20th century had arrived. Televisions were starting to appear in homes, whitegoods were liberating housewives and soon man would fly to the moon. Electricity was everywhere and the new age of invention was both exhilarating and accelerating.

Jack took mind of this technological revolution and decided that the way forward in the exploding post-war economy of steel and circuits and washing machines was, not to put too fine a point on it, wood. And so he took his half of the family fortune and ploughed it into a rundown woodyard next to the Dandenong railway line, which had, with no discernible irony, been recently electrified.

Younger readers may not know what a woodyard is – which in itself provides a clue to Jack's business acumen – but it is a simple proposition: It sells wood. Not, it must be stressed, any particular wood in any particular shape or of any particular quality that has been cut and shaped so that you might build something with it or make something out of it, as per the modern Bunnings variety. Nor indeed did it involve *a* wood in the sense of a forest composed of trees and such that would at least soak up some of the carbon from the boom times ahead. No, Jack's vision was to provide chopped up pieces of wood for people to set fire to, if for no other reason than there wasn't really much else you could do with it.

In my grandfather's defence, wood and the fire it brought forth had been an integral part of humankind's development for many thousands of years. However, most economists of the time agreed it was not necessarily the product of the future. Even in Dandenong, a humble country town on a recalcitrant road to suburbia, virtually every household had both electricity and gas, which were, as inexplicable as it might seem, fast becoming the heating and cooking methods of choice.

Adding to Jack's woes was the fact that even given the limitations of his star product, he was not a particularly good salesman. On many occasions he was simply not present at the woodyard. On the occasions he was there, he was more often than not drunk. And on one celebrated occasion he managed to combine the best of both worlds by arriving at the woodyard both late and drunk and accidentally driving his car into the vehicle of the only customer who happened to be there at the time.

Still, he was nothing if not quick on his feet. When the customer pointed out, quite reasonably, that Jack had just rear-ended his small flat-bed truck, my grandfather responded by observing that it was several minutes after midday on a Saturday.

'Technically,' he said, triumphantly peering at his watch, 'we're closed.'

Needless to say he struggled to finalise that particular sale.

In a marriage that was no more young nor foolish than any other of its day, Jack had wed my grandmother Irma, a shy girl from a farm outside a tiny town called Elmore born amid four sisters and a brother. She came to Dandenong for a job at the local telephone exchange only to be captivated by Jack's chiselled face and proud bearing at a local dance hall and subsequently bore him three children. Thereafter her life descended into an unanticipated whirlpool of frugality and chaos, however she stood like a praetorian guard over his failings, desperately fighting to maintain a veneer of respectability. This mostly comprised dying her hair a fierce natural black while raising two daughters and a son in what she hoped they would mistake for an orderly house.

Jack, too, had appearances to maintain. While he was vastly poorer than his working-class neighbours he always voted Liberal – he was, after all, a businessman. And despite being a chronic alcoholic he never once darkened the door of the Dandenong Workers Club, even though at some 200 metres from his home it was the closest available drinking establishment. Whatever privations his bad choices had delivered upon his family he never carried himself as the man he was, only the man he wished to be.

To this end he loved classical music, cryptic crosswords and books. For all that he could not deliver his children, he was resolute that it would be delivered nonetheless. He determined that they would each attend university just as he had longed to, and to his credit all three of them did. Admittedly this was only possible due to the free education revolution delivered by Gough Whitlam, who my grandfather repeatedly refused to vote for, but results are results.

Alongside my grandfather's high passions, heavy folly and hard drinking, my grandmother was, beneath her quiet heroism, an anxious and worried soul. Self-effacing and modest to the point of self-loathing, she also had a limitless heart and sharp wit but rarely the confidence or opportunity to express either – a life built on poverty and perpetual distress is not a strong launchpad for such gifts. Yet in the chasm that divided them, Jack and Irma, against all probability, raised three intelligent, decent and good-hearted children.

The eldest, Genevieve, was the spirited troublemaker. The youngest, John – or as my grandmother dubbed him 'John, John, greatest of all Johns' – was the timid and adored favourite. And there in the middle was my mother, Christine: quiet, introspective, selfless and – for reasons no science has had the care nor resources to fathom – pathologically fussy. This particularness took shape in everything from food (she refused to eat any ice-cream that wasn't Peters) to the little solitary activities she busied herself with. On one occasion she took it upon herself to produce a chart of all the flags of the world, carefully drawing each in the exact correct shape, colour and ensign. When she made a tiny error on the last one and tried to correct it, the eraser tore a hole in the page. No amount of Peters ice-cream could console her then.

It came as a surprise therefore, when, at the age of 24, after completing a diploma of education at Frankston Teachers College, this shy, self-contained and painstaking girl quietly but firmly packed up her meagre worldly belongings – including a collection of dresses she had sewn for herself – and moved to Laos, one of the world's more remote and improbable destinations. There she would meet and fall in love with a wandering American troubadour called Greg Hildebrand, a man with little to show for himself except one guitar and two divorces. And that is how I came to be.

Peace and War

If Oscar Wilde's great creation Lady Bracknell had been born a hundred years later she might have observed that to have one hippie parent is a misfortune. To have two looks like carelessness.

Thus was my beginning. My mother and father were married in Laos so that he could get visiting rights to her in hospital. It is one thing for a young Catholic girl to wed in a communist Southeast Asian outpost, another for that wedding to be to a twice-married folk singer from Colorado, and quite a third for the nuptials to be conducted solely for medicinal purposes. Futhermore, photographic evidence indicates both were wearing kaftans during the ceremony. It is difficult to envision a scenario that could be more wholly against God.

Were that not enough, allow me to rattle off some basic hippie pedigree. My father didn't just listen to Bob Dylan, he played on the same bill as him at Greenwich Village coffee houses. He went to real-life 'happenings'. He went to real-life 'peace-outs'. He and his friend 'Pilgrim' used to have 'freak-fests' in front of the targets at gun clubs to propagate non-violent conflict resolution. He lived with a group of beatniks in Boulder, Colorado – the home of *Mork and Mindy* no less – where they referred to themselves as 'The Tribe'. He then followed one of the tribeswomen to Sweden where they lived in a remote farmhouse and rode a bicycle for hours in the snow so he could buy organic farming equipment. And he was an erstwhile adherent of a man called 'Wavy Gravy', whose happenings were widely considered to be the best of all.

In other words, if you think you've seen a hippie then frankly you ain't seen shit.

My mother, on the other hand, was not so much an alpha-fuck-the-system-they-don't-understand-us-hippie but an at-one-with-everything-let's-make-the-world-a-better-place hippie. She communed with the whole world around her. Her dual specialities were the wonder of nature and anyone who was remotely impoverished or oppressed. Everything my mother encountered was either the greatest moral atrocity ever perpetuated or a deep metaphysical epiphany. She once described her own bowel movements as the gateway to a spiritual awakening, something no child should ever have to hear. To this day she still yearns for an outside toilet unconstrained by the man-made hegemony of walls.

Conversely, the only activities that my father found spiritually enlightening were playing music, watching television and sleeping until noon – all of which he excelled at. Everyday chores such as doing the dishes or the vacuuming seemed to elude him. Or rather, as my mother was later to observe, he seemed to elude them. When she asked him to mow the lawn once, he dismissed the suggestion by saying he refused to conform to a bourgeois middle-class social hierarchy. Certainly he achieved that.

Another middle-class ideal that my father eschewed was the notion that a man should have if not one wife then at least as few wives as possible. As noted, he had already acquired two ex-wives when he met and married my mother, but as she had gone directly from sleepy suburban Dandenong to the wilds of Indochina, this fact failed to set off the alarm bells that might have registered in someone who had spent time in, say, the real world. Even now my mother will still defend her marital choice on the basis that 'Greg had a first class mind' – although to be fair she has recently started using the past tense.

As this great and solitary compliment suggests, my mother inherited her mother's deep insecurity about her own intelligence. Partly for this reason – although more out of her unworldly altruism – my mother's all-consuming mantra was that intelligence and achievement might be all well and good, but the only thing that truly matters is the decency with which you live and behave towards others. And if you can find spiritual fulfilment in bowel movements, well, so much the better.

This might sound an almost banal philosophy were the benchmarks of what constituted decency not drawn up by my mother herself, in whose eyes Mother Teresa might have done something worthwhile in her life had she just tried a little harder. My mother's moral values were every bit as absolute as the laws of physics, although the punishment for falling foul of them was not as mercifully swift. Throughout my childhood every small problem I had – be it a splinter in my finger or a bicycle's flat tyre – would quickly be met with an excruciatingly long story about a woman from the swim club who was suffering from clinical bipolar while her firstborn son was in jail, her second had been in a motor vehicle accident and her daughter – did she forget to mention? – had cerebral palsy.

My mother had of course given them a couple of hundred dollars from her own meagre savings only to be dismayed when the woman squandered it on some sheets and pillows from Kmart when, as both her and I clearly knew, she could easily have bought the doona secondhand from an op shop and spent the money on something more genuinely necessary. Suffice to say, there are few people in the world who consider the purchase of low-cost bedding an extravagance.

By contrast my father had little capacity for self-denial. There was never any discernible sense of stoicism or duty or doing something simply because 'it's the right thing to do'. He was a free wheel. This is not to say that he was deliberately immoral; rather just that, like countless musicians before him, he was fundamentally a lazy narcissist who never particularly cared what anybody else thought. And when one doesn't care what anybody thinks the road to self-righteousness is paved with gold.

Of course other people's immorality consumed him. When the smallest perceived slight befell him he would explode into a wild rage of indignation. For a pacifist he had quite a temper.

On one occasion it exploded while he was performing at a coffee house in Melbourne and two women were talking at a volume that displeased him. He stopped singing, put down his guitar and started screaming at them from the stage. On another he flew into hysterics when a young supermarket cashier asked to check his bag, a condition of entering the store duly signposted at the entrance. This, my father later explained, was a gross invasion of his civil rights, and something to be fought against at all costs lest we descend into tyranny. I considered him a hero both times.

And to his credit my father was also occasionally able to get outraged on my behalf. When I was a young boy, maybe five years old, I developed an instant obsession with a cowboy shirt on display for a dollar or two at an op shop in Dandenong. Being a cruelly disenfranchised folk singer in the age before Eftpos and ATMs, my father didn't have that kind of cash on him so he asked the lady to put it aside for when we would return with our riches.

It was maybe days later when we'd got our finances in order that my father returned to collect the shirt, only to discover it had been sold to someone else. After the lady explained the mistake my father referred to her as a 'stupid bitch'.

Still, righteousness is an unpredictable serpent. Another time when we were in a small town in country Victoria making the obligatory op shop call I took a liking to an orange construction helmet. It was fifty cents and the sum of my dreams and even more miraculously my father happened to have that kind of cash on him that day. But when it came time to finalise the purchase it soon became apparent that we were the only people in the store. Even though the door was open and we had walked right in, there wasn't actually anyone there. My leaping heart was suddenly gripped by the cold damp claw of defeat. Clearly I would not be wearing my dream helmet that day.

Maybe my father sensed how important the hardhat was to me or maybe he just had no concept of capitalism's fundamental pillar that a transaction requires both a purchasor and a purchasee. Either way, before the tears could flow he simply said that we would take the hat and leave the money. He then made a grand show of counting out exactly fifty cents from the smaller denominations of coins in his pocket and placed them in a neat stack on the counter. The whole thing felt dangerously like stealing and I suggested that if we were going to go through with this course of action we should immediately flee the premises and make a dash for the car. However, Greg Hildebrand insisted that we would walk casually out with our heads held high. We had, after all, done nothing wrong – or at least that's what he wanted any witnesses to think. As we strutted out of the store, carefully closing the tingling door behind us, I had never felt more impressed by his courage and daring. I imagined our exploits captured in black and white newsprint: MY FATHER – THE GREAT OP SHOP ROBBER.

It only occurred to me years later that we may have been leaving behind a recently deceased little old lady decomposing in the storeroom, but no childhood is without its casualties.

Away from the legally ambiguous world of op shop heists my father did display some moral characteristics. He would often rail against broader injustices – even if it was rarely with the same fury as the ones that befell him, nor with any apparent intention of doing anything about them. The most passionate I can recall was a rather violent outburst against the Hawke government and how disgracefully right-wing it was – 'cosying up to that damn Rupert Murdoch'.

What particular outrage Bob Hawke had visited upon him was never clear and when it came down to talking about who he had voted for or which way he would vote again it emerged that the point was moot. Despite living in the country for a decade he had never bothered to become an Australian citizen.

Years later he expressed a similar disgust at a friend of his who specialised in tax avoidance and had purchased a handsome sports car and a nice house at which my father played in a series of regular 'music nights'. When I asked why he had not upbraided his friend for the abrogation of his fiscal duties to the state my father angrily blamed 'the system' for allowing him to do it. Outrage and action rarely joined forces in him. Personal responsibility came a distant third.

And yet I adored him, worshipped his every word and step. When I was very young we would often stay up late together watching television, the programs carefully chosen and plotted by his discerning critical eye – that *first class mind* my mother talked about so often.

Most fascinating was his great particularity. Even his laziness was carefully orchestrated with the precision of a great conductor. His TV watching was never haphazard. He always had a very deliberate reason for watching this show or that, each lucky winner circled with dark blue ink in the *Green Guide* – a television liftout in *The Age* to which he attributed almost supernatural powers. Of course he had his disagreements with it – there were, after all, enemies everywhere – but old comrades like Jim Schembri or other favoured reviewers would carry the day. Years later he would evolve this process into a finely calibrated system of index cards upon which he glued movie reviews accompanied by his own cursive notes and then filed alphabetically in an ever-increasing number of slender boxes slotted around the television. This was to be his proudest and greatest endeavour.

But back in my early childhood no cue cards were needed. His favourite program was a 1970s show called *Taxi* whose plotlines, jokes or overall point I never really understood – although I was, in my defence, only four or five years old. But I did understand a greater truth. *Taxi* would come on somewhere around midnight and I knew if I was with him in the lounge room then that I had really made it. Not only had I broken through to the magical world of *staying up late* but when the credits rolled at the end there was always a good chance that he would take me for a walk to the 7-Eleven where he would buy a litre of milk for the next day – a small contribution towards his household duties – and might also weaken at the counter and purchase a Bertie Beetle for me. At that moment no child was ever happier.

But outside those precious bubbles the real world still swirled and heaved. And with such obvious disinterest in the feelings of checkout chicks and elderly op shop ladies, it is little wonder that my father showed a similar obliviousness to the feelings of my mother. Or perhaps it was merely the same disregard he had for anyone's feelings when they failed to coalign with his own. Either way, he soon commenced an affair with his banjo student. Her name was Joy, and she remains one of history's most ironically christened individuals.

The romance began in the 'music room' of our small Dandenong home, an otherwise small and innocuous third bedroom in which my father took a handful of students for lessons one night a week. Yearning to be a part of this mysterious other dimension, I would often lie on the carpet outside, listening to the instruments and voices through the crack underneath the door. But my young ears failed to detect the true nature of his latest duet.

With trademark honesty – to his credit he was never considerate enough to be a liar – my father informed my mother about the whole thing and one night he gently interrupted one of my regular Lego sessions to tell me he had something to say: He was leaving.

As with everything my father told me when he wasn't caught by one of his childlike rages, this was explained in a measured, reasoned and wholly rational way. He would be leaving the house, he would still come back twice a week, and really it would be a better deal for everybody. In response I started crying uncontrollably and told him he simply couldn't go. After pausing for thought, my father said that if that was the way I felt about it he supposed maybe he could stay for a few more months if he had to. Even as I spilled tears onto the plastic bricks in front of me I could sense his disappointment and I too felt ashamed that I hadn't dealt with the situation with the appropriate level of thoughtful restraint. Surely at six years old I ought to have been more mature about the whole thing.

The situation that that moment gave birth to must have been unbearable for my mother, however for the sake of her firstborn son she accepted it with her usual grace. The deal was this: Greg would continue to live in the house and sleep, aptly enough, in the music room, while maintaining his right to continue his relationship with Joy. In return for this my mother would be allowed to continue to cook his meals and raise his children.

It's fair to say that the negotiation skills on the maternal side of the family had not much improved through the generations.

On one particular night, however, even my mother's seemingly unbreakable stoicism gave way. My sister, barely a year old, was crying on her arm, I was running around the house and my brother was convulsing wildly on the floor.

Greg, meanwhile, was sprucing himself up in front of the bathroom mirror in cheerful preparation for another date with Joy.

'Well, I'm off,' he said chirpily and made for the door.

Standing in the cluttered hallway across from him, my mother observed that while she was willing to tolerate his flagrant infidelity most nights of the week, tonight was just a little more flagrant and infidelious than most. Perhaps tonight, she ventured, he might be better placed to attend to his parenting duties.

'Now come on Christine,' my father said, obviously just trying to be reasonable. 'We had a *deal*.'

Here arrived what might be described as a moment of clarity. If the sight and sound of his own children howling and flailing on the ground wasn't going to move my father, it was obvious that a rational debate was also unlikely to do the job. And so my mother took a deep breath, drew back her shoulders, and punched my father in the face.

It says something about Greg Hildebrand's unassailable sense of self-importance, if not his first class mind, that even while suffering from major concussion he was able to recast any situation around him so as to entirely serve his own interests. Staggering back with the force of the blow and with the chaos of his own children still caterwauling all around, his omnipresent temper was suddenly nowhere to be seen.

'Well,' he said calmly, 'I can't stay now. There's violence in the home.'

And with that, he was gone.

The Second Son

Greg's dramatic exit left my mother alone to bring up me, my baby sister and my younger brother, who even by five years of age was approaching the prime of his life for mischief making.

His name was Patrick James Hildebrand and we all knew him as Paddy. He was born a year and two months after me yet by my mother's careful log of his development he was at each step more advanced than her adored eldest child, as outrageous as that might seem. He crawled, then walked, then talked, then read, all at an incredibly early age. It wasn't until he was about three years old that my mother noticed the change.

At first it was just small things, as one might expect from a small person. A lack of comprehension at what was going on, sudden mood swings, unpredictable outbursts of violence. All qualities not uncommon to any three-year-old child but my mother, having charted his precocious course since birth, knew that something was wrong.

But it was the turn of the 1980s, which in Melbourne might as well have been the 1950s. As she was bounced around from GPs to specialists to psychiatrists, desperately trying to explain Paddy's strange new behaviour, it became clearer and clearer that the doctors simply did not believe her. In a Kafkaesque demonstration of social insanity, the more convinced and insistent she became, the less they listened to her. Eventually, she later discovered, the file notes after one consultation suggested not that my brother be tested for mental incapacity but that my mother should be.

After years of fighting, my mother's madness prevailed and my brother was eventually diagnosed with a condition dubbed Lennox–Gastaut syndrome. For want of a better medical diagnosis, let us consult the 21st century's physician of choice, Dr Google. That font of all knowledge Wikipedia describes it thus:

Lennox–Gastaut syndrome (LGS) is a difficult-to-treat form of childhood-onset epilepsy that most often appears between the second and sixth year of life, and is characterized by frequent seizures and different seizure types; it is often accompanied by developmental delay and psychological and behavioral problems … Daily multiple seizures are typical … larger than that of any other epileptic syndrome … The seizures can cause sudden falling and/or loss of balance, which is why patients often wear a helmet to prevent head injury. In addition to daily multiple seizures of various types, children with LGS frequently have arrested/slowed psycho-motor development and behavior disorders.

In short, no one knows what the fuck it is. Nor what causes it, nor how it can be effectively treated. It is a monster in the shadows, a collection of symptoms in search of a disease.

As you might imagine, raising a child like this presented what modern parlance might term some 'unique challenges' and 'atypical childhood experiences'.

One example is that for the first few years of our lives Paddy and I shared a bedroom, in which I – being the naturally ordained heir – of course had the top bunk. We would therefore while away the hours between bedtime and sleep with a simple yet invigorating game involving me dangling my legs over the edge of my bed and Paddy, thrashing about in the bunk below, seeing how often he could bite them.

We both considered this pastime perfectly normal and it must be said that whatever other developmental delays Paddy had, there was certainly nothing lacking within this particular skill set. Every night he would regularly succeed in locking his jaws around my big toe or a tender calf muscle – although getting him to release the relevant body part was something he was apparently less adept at.

And so the normal parameters of playtime were completely foreign to Paddy, not to mention those who ever encountered him. Readers of a certain age may recall the great backyard shrine of the totem tennis pole and the heavy plastic yellow bats used to whack its stringed ball in either direction. Suffice to say when the game was played with Paddy it was not just the ball that got belted into submission. In yet another testament to his ingenuity he also soon discovered that a more competitive advantage could be exacted by turning the bat sideways and swiftly applying its rock-hard edge to the other player's bones.

On one occasion I foolishly let my guard down only to receive a cracking blow flush between the shoulder blades. I still remember the sound of the air whistling past the mighty weapon just before it landed on my spine, instantly distributing pain impulses to extremities of my body I scarcely knew existed. He was nothing if not a formidable opponent.

Even such incidents as these were a relatively easy escape. Slightly more enervating was when, after some forgotten provocation, Paddy cornered me around the side of the house with a sharpened axe. This, I realised, was a potentially serious situation. While I could usually best him at hand-to-hand combat, his innovative use of weaponry was, as we have seen, impressive to say the least. And while even the most impulsive child could usually be reasoned out of a potentially murderous course of action, it was difficult to talk Paddy down from the ledge when his blood was up.

After several impassioned pleas, threats and cries for help I came to accept that nothing was going to stop him from attempting to cleave me in two. And there was no means of escape. The side gate was locked behind me and any attempt to turn around and unlock it would surely be met with the same sensation between my shoulder blades I had already recently experienced via the totem tennis bat but this time with somewhat longer-lasting consequences.

And so I sighed, planted my feet on the spot and exhorted him to take his best shot.

Thankfully Paddy obliged, and reared the giant axe back over his shoulder with all his might so as to decapitate me in one fell swoop. In the tiny moment of truth when the axe lay primed behind him I was able to dart around and pull it down and away from both our young torsos. Thus disarmed, my brother moaned resignedly that I had ruined his fun and, after a few shakes of the axe on my part, scurried off to find another implement with which to dispose of me.

The True Believers

It was a sunny and otherwise unremarkable afternoon in Dandenong as I walked home from school, through our open front door and into the bathroom. Thereupon I saw a bearded naked man towelling himself off with cheerful vigour, which even in our house was less than usual.

'You must be Joey!' he exclaimed, and ruffled the hair on my head.

Clearly he had been backgrounded more thoroughly than I had.

Hearing this unexpected introduction, my mother came rocketing in from another room and propelled me into the kitchen, whereupon I was hurriedly offered any kind of food I could possibly dream of. To her dismay I was not so easily distracted.

'Who's the guy in the bathroom, Mum?' I asked matter-of-factly.

'Well,' my mother replied, as though her next words would explain everything, 'that's Don.'

After my father left my mother had taken up long-distance running, the first step in her emerging new conviction that the only way one could ever hope to enjoy life was to put oneself through extreme physical pain. In my case the pain involved meeting the various men in her running club who seemed to take a very healthy interest in my mother's athleticism. My mother obviously took this to be yet more evidence of the collective human joy that was aroused by physical exercise, however I couldn't help but feel many of her male friends had a different kind of arousal in mind.

As it happened, the only person in the running club more innocent in such matters was Don himself, which makes it all the sweeter an irony that he was the one who ended up naked in my bathroom. Despite being 42 years old he still lived at home with his mother and had his whole life been the possessor of just one job, as a draftsman for the State Electricity Commission.

This may sound like an unremarkable occupation but it was integral to our newfound friendship. My whole faith system to this point – and even, if I am honest, to this day – was predicated on the belief that Superman was real and every spare waking moment of my childhood was spent drawing up my own comic books depicting him and other superheroes in various states of gallantry and intergalactic detective work. Don may never have fully understood my love of Superman or how it framed the world as I saw it but he understood it enough to present me once a week with a mechanical pencil he had pilfered from the stationery cupboard.

My only previous experience with such advanced technology was the occasional overpriced Pacer I could convince my grandfather to buy me on one of his drunk days. Now I had a man who was offering architect-grade drawing pencils for free – the kind you couldn't even get in newsagents. There was no limit to the superheroes I could draw with such a weapon, and their ever-escalating headquarters would be impenetrable with the number of levels and computer consoles I could now deliver. Never had a man become so close to being a god.

Don was a simple man and he was also a good man. There was nothing he wouldn't do for my mother or her kids, provided it was within his albeit sometimes limited capabilities. Just a trip to the pool or the park – or indeed the occasional mechanical pencil – would be more than enough to keep us gratefully entertained and give my mother some much-needed respite.

Such easy and thoughtless generosity immediately set him apart from my father's painstakingly premeditated de facto parenting. Under the deal struck upon the divorce he was to see us two evenings a week but did so only under an ever-expanding set of conditions which were as carefully constructed to benefit him as they were to present the guise of benefiting us.

At first he would come and see us on his own but soon complained that this left his newly acquired wife, Joy, all alone in their house – and surely we kids wouldn't want that? So Joy soon started to come along too and we would engage in the traditional divorced dad routine of hanging out at the park and going to McDonald's – the ultimate weapon in any parental war. Then when those activities reached the end of their brief natural lifespan my father would deposit us home while Joy waited in the car. And just as surely when we questioned this state of affairs my father explained that for some quibbling reason or another my mother felt less than comfortable about his erstwhile mistress entering her house. Naturally I protested this injustice to my mother and soon the visits involved he and Joy both coming over and staying two evenings a week while Chrissy was obliged to vacate her own home.

By contrast Don was overjoyed to have stumbled across the family life that had so long eluded him and could not have embraced his duties with more unconditional glee. These unthinking kindnesses had guaranteed my mother's eternal affection and gratitude but sadly they could not guarantee her love. There was what my mother described as a disconnect in 'a meeting of the minds', as careful a euphemism as she could muster. Over the course of several years I repeatedly asked my mother why she hadn't married Don – as surely all grown-ups were supposed to do. Eventually, having exhausted every other tactical euphemism and evasion she simply sighed and said, 'Well, you see darling, he votes Liberal.'

At last everything became clear. Even at the age of ten I had been a Labor man for years. My political awakening had begun on a Saturday night in March 1983 when my father, mother and I were gathered in the lounge as the election results came rolling in on our brand new National television. This was an unprecedented technological marvel that had been recently installed in the centre of the room, where it now stood upon its proud chipboard legs. Anything it broadcast was bound to be of great importance.

The names the television poured forth from its small metallic speaker were also familiar to me. Only a few weeks earlier I had heard my father angrily pontificate about the gross injustice of the upstart Bob Hawke rolling

Bill Hayden for the ALP leadership just as an unsuspecting Malcolm Fraser was driving to Yarralumla to call the poll. I naturally assumed that these were all friends of his and that Bob Hawke must have been a very bad friend indeed. My father also seemed to dislike Malcolm Fraser but for some reason not with the same passion. The only one of the three he had kind words for was Bill Hayden, but according to the television Bill Hayden wasn't very important anymore. This only seemed to make my father angrier still.

In the days leading up to that Saturday the National TV was awash with ads whose primary discernible difference was a logo with one crumpled Australian flag marked 'Australian Labor Party' in an old-fashioned Times New Roman font compared to a logo with three slightly futuristic Australian flags perfectly slotted into an 'L' shape with the word 'Liberal' inserted next to them in bold capital letters. Finally a single image had managed to combine my love of Lego with my love of superhero lettering. I was sitting entranced when my mother came into the room.

'I think I like the Liberals, Mum,' I said.

My mother's pupils shrank in horror and she almost fell back outside the door.

'What on Earth would make you say something like that?' she said.

I explained to her how the letters sat together just like the Superman masthead and the three flags sat perfectly conjoined. For a moment I thought she was going to call for an ambulance.

'Why?' I asked. 'What's wrong?'

'Well,' she said, 'the thing is the Liberals look after the rich people and Labor looks after the poor people.'

'Oh,' I said. 'And are we rich?'

'No darling,' she said. 'We're poor.'

This last statement didn't fill me with any shock or disappointment – it wasn't as though I was struck by a sense of political disenfranchisement or class oppression. Being six years old I never had any money anyway. It was my parents who were the gatekeepers of untold riches that they constantly withheld from me at crucial moments in milk bars.

It was just a simple fact I had previously been unaware of but now knew: I was poor and I was Labor.

A week or two later when the National television began declaring that the ALP was leading in the count my conviction could not have been stronger. I was sitting on the floor so enraptured by the frenzied voices coming from the TV screen and the unified happiness it excited in my warring parents – even Greg allowed himself some satisfaction, as though despite his reservations he had personally delivered a landslide for Labor – that I had even been distracted from my precious Lego. When it came time for me to go to bed I was devastated to discover that not only was the final result still not in but the truck I had been so painstakingly constructing throughout the night remained unfinished.

Despite protesting both injustices, I was sent off to my room on the strict condition that when the count was finished I was to be immediately informed.

Hours later in the middle of the night, I felt my mother's presence in the room as she came to check that I was tucked up as promised. Through half-shut eyes and tired lips I managed to murmur just two words: 'Who won?'

'We did, darling,' my mother cooed as she stroked my head. 'We did.'

The next morning I awoke to discover the Lego truck I had been working on was sitting next to my bed, mysteriously completed in the night by some unknown force.

My God, I thought. This new Labor government really gets things done.

My Grandmother the Drug Dealer

Don was not capable of understanding such ideological passions himself, nor indeed in others. Even the basest pragmatism of politics, the otherwise unconquerable law of mutual self-interest, effortlessly eluded him. For as long as we had known him he had been a draftsman for the State Electricity Commission, the epitome of a lifelong public service bureaucrat. Yet he steadfastly voted Liberal until one day the party he had so long supported finally won office, sold off the SEC and made him redundant.

Having said that, he did make off with a giant payout that left him considerably wealthier than his newly adopted family, so perhaps he was wiser than all of us. But even these riches couldn't buy my mother's hand in marriage. To win that he would have had to tell her he voted Labor, something Don was never wise, wily or dishonest enough to do.

But simple minds breed simple dreams and simple dreams are often the best. If my mother liked him a little bit for taking her kids on little trips, he reasoned, imagine how much she would like him if he took us on a great big one.

So began the fermentation of an idea for Don to take the whole family on a three-month odyssey around the country, abandoning the comfortable mores of suburban Melbourne for the wide Australian outback and beyond. This journey through the harsh antipodean landscape was to be undertaken in our white Mazda van, a bottom-of-the-line two-wheel-drive piece of sheet metal that wasn't even intended to have passengers in the back seat, let alone plough through desert floodplains. Don was confident he could absolve these problems by dubbing the van 'Betsy' and talking to it encouragingly from time to time. Likewise, the expedition was to be helmed by my mother and Don, neither of whom had any outback survival skills. Indeed Don, as previously mentioned, was yet to even experience moving out of his mother's house.

And yet, ominous as all these signs might have been, none was as singularly inauspicious as the fact that on the eve of our departure my grandmother had just been prosecuted for drug possession.

While I may have been only eight years old at the time, I did increasingly have a sense that my family was not entirely conventional. However it always consoled my young heart that none of us had done any jail time.

The problem had started, as so many problems among our clan apparently did, when one of us committed the unpardonable sin of having the prospect of some success. In this case it was my uncle Johnny, my grandparents' youngest child and only son, who was wholly adored for this reason alone, all others being rendered immediately irrelevant.

Being a shy, diligent and devoted child my mother had, upon returning from her improbable Asian adventure, moved barely 500 metres from her childhood home, making her the first point of care and contact for her ageing parents and she was appropriately rewarded with the assumed nonchalance that proximity always brings. Never one to be so ensnared, the eldest child Genevieve literally fled to the hills in order to prove she was perfectly capable of having a dysfunctional family on her own. Meanwhile the beloved and evergreen Johnny moved to the hip Melbourne beachside suburb of St Kilda, a place of unimaginable glamour and vice for a family whose usual idea of decadence was a grocery shop that stayed open past 5pm.

There Johnny became involved in local politics, joining a community action group called Turn the Tide dedicated to fighting high-rise overdevelopment along St Kilda's Esplanade strip. To everybody's surprise, not least the protesters' themselves, the movement was so successful that several of them got elected to council, whereupon they promptly nominated Johnny for mayor. Needless to say the local newspaper article recording his elevation moved at light speed from the printing press to a frame atop my grandmother's television, where it stayed until her dying day.

Johnny was, to say the least, an unconventional government leader. A telling example is that his car – a rusted-out 1964 American Rambler, which he had coloured turquoise with some leftover housepaint – was so thoroughly unroadworthy that after his first commute to Town Hall it sat immovable in the mayoral car spot until some civic-minded ratepayers were recruited to push it away.

A less unique aspect of his political career was that, like most of his constituents, he didn't mind a puff of a joint now and then. And not wanting, for obvious public relations reasons, to be part of an underground drug ring he decided to grow his own marijuana. The only catch was that it was difficult to cultivate even a modest personal crop in St Kilda's highly urbanised environment – a situation, I should stress, that was in no way linked to his own celebrated efforts to ease housing density. And so he did what all good boys do and asked his mother for help.

As far as my grandmother was concerned he might as well have asked if he could put a bullet in her head or borrow 50 cents for the parking meter. The answer was always going to be the same: 'Of course, darling.'

The question of whether my grandfather Jack would have been so accommodating remains academic. Had he been sober enough at any point to have been asked, he certainly wouldn't have remained that way long enough to remember his answer. Still, as politicians are constantly discovering to their detriment, a lack of consultation inevitably begets disaster.

And so it was that my grandfather placed a classified ad in the newspaper for the sale of his beloved EJ Holden. After many years of loyal and often illegal service at his drunken hands, it was time to let go.

When it came to car ownership, it is fair to say that the phrase 'like father, like son' aptly applied. It was not from nowhere that my uncle acquired his natural instinct for automotive disregard. The Holden might have been as proud as its owner but it was also as deeply flawed. At best it might have yielded fifty bucks from a scrapyard; at worst my grandfather could have given them the fifty just to take it away. In either case it would have been a deal well struck.

But affection cannot be measured in money and so the price Jack was asking for the vehicle was an absurdly high sum calculated on the basis of all the good times he'd had in it rather than, say, what the car was actually worth.

When prospective buyers approached the house, most, upon glimpsing the rusted brown carcass beside it, sensibly elected to just keep driving. Unfortunately one bargain hunter was not so decisive.

The precise metrics of Jack's condition that day are unknown, but it is a reliable assumption that when he answered the door he was drunk. And, like the rest of us, when he was drunk he talked shit.

He took the man to the car and presented it with wide open arms, as though he'd just revealed the Batmobile. However there were certain clues that the Holden was not quite the mint condition collector's item the ad had suggested it to be. The most obvious was that while elsewhere on the lawn the grass had been cut to a manageable height, on the patch of driveway where the Holden sat, the blades were knee-high. It didn't take Batman to figure out that this car hadn't gone anywhere for a while.

Despite this initial seemingly insurmountable disaster, things still managed to get worse. Upon inspecting the interior of the car, whose torn upholstery and cracked dashboard should already have made any further scrutiny redundant, the buyer took the notion to peel back the floormats, which had hitherto been fused to the base of the car by years of accumulated grime.

In Jack's defence he had been unaware that the floormats were movable objects, and so when their removal revealed giant holes in the bottom of the car he was no doubt genuinely surprised. However it was the fact that grass was actually growing through these holes that caused the visitor's mood to, in my mother's careful words, 'change perceptibly'.

'Well, I don't know about the car,' he said tersely. 'But you've certainly got plenty of grass.'

Sensing a new avenue of appeal through which to close the sale, my grandfather replied with renewed enthusiasm, 'Oh yes, we love our grass here. In fact as you can see we have lots of plants.'

Thereupon he once more spread his arms open wide and gestured to the whole backyard, whose vista at this point happened to include three large budding marijuana bushes poking out from behind the shed.

'Yes,' he nodded, with a warm smile. 'We really love our plants.'

The buyer never did come back, however the police most certainly did. When my grandmother answered the door she was shocked but not surprised. And for the first time in her life she was grateful that Jack had once more disappeared from the house, nowhere to be seen.

'Alright,' she said, anxious to get it over with before he returned. 'Take me in.'

Among his finer parenting moments, my father had always assured me that Victorian cops were the kind who only offered you your first phone call after they'd belted you with the phone book. But whatever their particular obsession with the *Yellow Pages* the charging of my grandmother with the possession and cultivation of cannabis was the most reluctant prosecution ever undertaken by a police force in Australia's history.

Even so, and with suspicious enthusiasm, the adults in my family took great pride in the fact that the old lady never squealed. Johnny was not just her delicate doe-eyed favourite but he was also running for mayor and, it was decided, she couldn't possibly allow his campaign to be despoiled by a drug scandal. I could almost imagine the relief around the kitchen table as her three adult children all nodded their heads and agreed she wouldn't have to be whacked.

Of course the cops knew she was growing it for someone else. Even in 1980s Dandenong a 70-something churchgoing grandmother didn't quite fit the profile of a hardened drug dealer. And there was also the fact that, during their frustrated attempts to question her, it emerged she clearly had little idea what marijuana actually was. Confession-wise, this grated with the notion that she'd grown it all for her own insatiable appetite for the devil's lettuce. Ultimately she just kept telling the investigating officers how terribly sorry and embarrassed she was, and they kept telling her how terribly sorry and embarrassed they were too.

When it came before the magistrate he could only concur, being every bit as confused as the prosecution as to what my grandmother was doing in court in the first place. He abruptly gave her a three-month good behaviour bond which, he generously opined, she did not seem to be in any danger of breaching. This was greeted with great relief by her three children, not least of all Johnny, who had well-founded fears for his mortal soul had the decision gone the other way.

Meanwhile, back at the house Don and I were busy packing the van with all our worldly belongings, accompanied by Annie's excitable chirps and Paddy's excitable eye-gouging. I had managed to gather that in recent weeks there had been some uncertainty about the trip but my mother had always been evasive on the subject, as the offspring of druglords are no doubt conditioned to be. On this day, however, she had mysteriously disappeared on some important errand in town and so I seized the opportunity to quiz Don.

'So Don, are we *really* going all around Australia?' I asked.

'I think so,' he replied, stacking a battery powered fridge in the van. 'We've just got to find out if your grandmother's going to jail.'

This, perhaps unsurprisingly, was one of the things my mother had expressly told Don *not* to say. However telling Don not to say something was as ambitious as giving a flight manual to a can of apricots and asking it to land a plane.

And so when my mother rounded the front gate that afternoon I was a distraught young man. As hardy as young children might be, they rarely want to see their grandparents do any serious prison time.

'What's happened to Irma?' I asked her urgently. 'Is it true she's going to jail?'

After shooting a quick damning look at Don, who absorbed it with his usual oblivion, my mother turned back towards me with her most earnest, sorrowful face. For someone whose whole life was dedicated to earnestness and sorrow this was as powerful an expression of tragedy as a human could convey.

'Don't worry darling,' she said tenderly. 'She'll be out by the time we get back.'

In an instant my whole body turned liquid and the tears that were flooding my eyes were just water upon water. Then the air rushed in and circuited my heaving chest until it burst forth again in a mournful animal howl: 'NOOOOOOO!!!!!!!!'

My mother gave me a warm forever hug and then turned to walk inside the house as I stood soaking the front lawn with my tears, while Don looked on perplexed.

'Hang on Chris,' he said, glancing anxiously towards the van he had so diligently packed as instructed. 'That's not what you said on the phone.'

My mother turned back, her eyes twinkled and she burst out laughing.

'Oh gawd,' she said with a giant grin. 'It's fine. She got off. She's back at home waiting for us right now.'

For a saintly, nurturing, nature-loving pacifist my mother always did have a deeply fucked-up sense of humour.

As I collapsed in her arms sobbing new tears of relief Don strode up to the two of us trembling with frustration.

'Look, just be straight with me Chris,' he said. 'Is she going to jail or not?'

The Wide Brown Land

It was an indication of our family's modest expectations that the mere avoidance of jail was considered a promising omen. And so we packed up the van and embarked on our transcontinental roadtrip full of thoroughly ill-founded optimism. Even Don felt confident that road signs whose large menacing letters declared 'FOUR WHEEL DRIVE ONLY' were simply intended to be guidelines.

The first leg of the journey from Melbourne to Ballarat was a relatively uncontroversial one, especially once I discovered that the caravan we were staying in had a television in it. However as we ventured deeper into the red centre there appeared to be a growing disconnect between the roads we were driving on – and it must be stressed I use the word 'roads' in the loosest possible sense – and the vehicle we were driving on them with.

This juxtaposition came to a head when my mother and Don decided that for reasons of national pride or spiritual awakening we were called upon to visit Lake Eyre, Australia's vast fabled inland sea. But of course, being Australian, it is a recalcitrant sea, only filling with water every quarter-century or so. As we headed inland through

South Australia my mother regaled us with tales of the incredible flocks of water birds that would descend upon the lake's sacred shores and feast upon the fish washed down from the rivers in those precious rare years of the high flood. I was mesmerised. For the first time in my life I got a sense of just how big, how beautiful and how unforgiving this country could be.

'Wow,' I said, as she filled my head with images of clouds of pelicans and sandpipers and silver gulls undulating above the water. 'And is this one of those years?'

'No,' she said. 'It isn't.'

Not to be dissuaded by such trifling distinctions, Don set good old Betsy on a course to the great salt basin, driving along rock, sand and almost every other surface known to man barring that which could be categorised as anything resembling a road. The four-cylinder van was as overloaded as it was under-motored and had no four-wheel drive nor off-road tyres. The closest thing it had to a life-saving feature was my mother's chicken sandwiches, and even they were running out.

While driving along these hundreds of kilometres of desert road we had already been bogged several times but had managed to get out of it through the tried and true method of digging out the sand beneath the rear wheels and replacing it with bracken, one of mother nature's most practical species of fauna. But rather than turning back we instead took each successful escape attempt as proof of our infallible outback survival skills and a sign that we should keep pressing further inland.

For legal purposes, I should stress that when I say 'we' I am referring to Don and a war council of children aged eight, seven and two. After the first apprehension my mother had been steadfastly urging Don to turn around and go back before we got bogged again and ended up stuck in the middle of the desert with nobody around for thousands of kilometres to help us. And of course when we did get bogged again and ended up stuck in the middle of the desert with nobody around for thousands of kilometres to help us, Don naturally blamed my mother.

Despite all the bracken in the world, there was nothing to be done. The van was stuck with its chassis flat on the ground and four piles of sand around it where the wheels used to be. My mother did her best to conceal from us any sense of danger but as the hours rolled by and her and Don's conversations became more and more heated I started to wonder if perhaps this wasn't a planned stop after all. For one thing there wasn't a McDonald's for miles.

Eventually dusk started to seep down on the once endless horizons and that was when the threat set in. In daylight anything is possible; at night-time everything is final. My mother was deeply worried, I could see that now. Even Don was more confused than usual. Great, I thought. First Burke and Wills and now us.

I was quietly preparing myself for death when a faint hum arose in the distant twilight and soon the red earth started to groan. At first it was just grains of sand buzzing on the surface and then the whole ground began to rumble. Don and Chrissy turned back to face the shrinking road we'd come along that now vaguely needled into nothingness. We younger ones looked to the sky, anticipating some kind of apocalypse. When nothing emerged from either direction we all turned ahead to the invisible lure of Lake Eyre. There upon the red-earth road we wondered how our country's fickle heart, which had defeated so many explorers before us, might exact one more vengeance this day.

Then the ground shook harder, the roar grew louder and against the half-light upon the horizon dark shapes grew larger as they bore down upon us.

'Good God, Don,' my mother yelled. 'What the Hell is it?'

'Well I'm not quite sure, Chris,' Don called back, squinting through the dust, 'but I think it's the army.'

As seemed to happen improbably often in his life, Don was completely correct. My mother was about to tell him to stop being an idiot when an entire battalion of the Australian Army rumbled up towards us and drew to a halt. In what seemed like a matter of seconds, and without any words I could discern, they attached a couple of steel cables to a truck, plucked the van from its sandy grave and swung it around 180 degrees in the direction my mother had insisted it should have been going in the first place.

'Geez, lucky you blokes came along,' Don said, as though he'd just passed them the football for a winning goal.

'Luck doesn't even cover it mate,' a sergeant told him gruffly as he climbed back into the truck. 'We only come out here once a year.'

The gravity of this statement bypassed Don in much the same way that asteroids bypass the Earth. As far as he was aware he was a mighty adventurer whose only slight hiccup in his bold itinerary had been duly remedied by the Australian Defence Force – which, after all, was what his taxes had been paying for all these years. Plus he got the chance to shoot the breeze with his comrades in arms, with whom he clearly shared a deep fellowship.

My mother, on the other hand, had been beside herself with fear and spent the rest of the long drive to the nearest campground oscillating between calming words towards us and silence towards Don. My sister and brother, by turns too young and too retarded to know what was really happening, had been thrilled by the noise and excitement and were still electrified to the point where their seatbelts could barely contain them.

I, meanwhile, felt quietly vindicated. My whole life I had believed with religious certainty in the existence of superheroes, an unstoppable and ever-vigilant legion of protectors sworn to uphold goodness and defend the vulnerable from danger. Everyone I had ever known, child and adult alike, had always insisted they weren't real, that there was no such thing. And yet here, in our darkest hour of need, and against every law of probability – I had heard what the sergeant said – the Australian Army had spontaneously appeared to deliver us from certain death.

It could not have been more clear. Heroes were real. Miracles were real. There were great and mysterious forces everywhere. The only question was whether you found them or they found you.

Fighting Fires

When you have a brother like Paddy there is a reason you need to believe in saviours. Few people in the world ever needed so much saving.

Towards the end of our continental circumnavigation we found ourselves in Cairns wandering aimlessly around a patioed 1970s-style shopping centre, as all travellers in Australia must inevitably do. While we lazily dispersed, hoping to find some entertainment among the half-closed hairdressers and tourist trinket shops, Paddy found a much more enlivening pursuit thanks to a hose reel he'd spotted in the courtyard. Like any self-respecting young boy Paddy had always fancied himself as a fireman and so he quickly slipped out of formation, grabbed the nozzle, turned on the tap and started spraying all potential sources of combustion – which naturally included the occasional shopfront – with enthusiastic diligence. Eventually one shopkeeper took exception to Paddy's unusually foresightful approach to fire prevention and started hurling abuse at him.

It was at this point that I discovered superheroes don't always wear capes, nor even khaki. In Don's case it seemed they wore parasilk tracksuit pants and gelled running shoes.

Unfortunately Don's only superpower was the ability to shout angrily, which he deployed against the shopkeeper to the effect that my younger brother was *'not right in the head!'* The shopkeeper, still unconvinced he had been bettered, continued to remonstrate. At this point Don adjudged that the situation needed further clarification and so strode up to the shopkeeper in his doorway and explained once more in a loud voice that Paddy was *'not right in the head!'* However this time he thoughtfully accompanied it with the suggestion that perhaps the shopkeeper shared the same condition.

The shopkeeper paused to consider this advice and then responded by punching Don in the face.

This single act had the dual effect of sending Don's dentures flying to places to which they were clearly not designed to go and attracting the attention of my mother and I, who, along with my two-year-old sister, were already feeling that we'd seen enough opals for one day. Grabbing her two non-brain-damaged children, Chrissy hauled us to the offending store, which Don had now entered with even more questions to be answered, namely 1) The unfinished business of why the shopkeeper had been yelling at Paddy; and 2) Why the shopkeeper had knocked his false teeth out.

We crossed the rubicon to find Don's fury had taken him deep inside a cheap souvenir shop and up against the back counter, behind which the shopkeeper had retreated, decidedly less certain of his supremacy over the wild tracksuited man before him. Don too knew he had the upper hand just not what to do with it.

Then, overtaken by either inspiration or instinct, it struck him. Don turned on his heels in an improbably elegant pirouette and extended his arms to the side, as though in pointed homage to the gold crucifix on the shopkeeper's chest. Thus positioned he strode back towards the door as his flattened palms collected every precious figurine on the shelves either side – I seem to remember an unusually large number of porcelain cows were casualties – and sent them hurtling towards the tiles below.

It did not take long for the shopkeeper's jaw to join his shattered merchandise on the floor as Don powered through his stock like a tsunami. For a man who loved capitalism so much he certainly knew how to strike at the heart of it.

My mother and I stood there gazing at Don with, it must be presumed, differing levels of admiration as he continued his march. Meanwhile Paddy just looked longingly at the hose.

Once outside Don looked back in disbelief, as though we had all suddenly deviated from the long-agreed plan.

'Well, what are you waiting for?' he said. *'Run!'*

And so, accompanied by the echo of shattering ceramics and the shopkeeper's mournful screams, we sprinted towards the white van parked around the corner. Don leapt into the driver's seat, turned on the ignition and flattened the accelerator at once and was in the process of driving away as my mother galloped alongside, flung her three children through the sliding door and hoisted herself into the front passenger seat in one surprisingly fluid movement.

After we'd nailed the first kilometre in sixty seconds flat we realised we'd shot past the caravan park we'd been staying in and the squat white buildings of Cairns were shrinking in the rear-view mirror.

'What do we do now Chris?' Don asked through his newly bared gums.

'Oh for fuck's sake, Don,' she said. 'Just drive.'

He dutifully obeyed and we floored it out of town, as happy as any five people in the world. For the first time in history our family had almost won a fight.

The System

In the latter part of the 20th century it became clear to all parties involved that the children of hippies did not fare well in the mainstream education system. This led many people to come to the conclusion that there was something wrong with the education system. Of course by the time everyone realised the problem was in fact that there was something wrong with the hippies it was all far too late.

The baseline problem is this: When you are raised by freaks you naturally become a freak and so to you the freaks who raised you seem perfectly normal. And if you do happen to meet anyone else it's almost always via your parents and so who are they likely to be? That's right: more fucking freaks.

To put it in scientific terms, we are talking about an experiment in which there is something deeply, deeply wrong with the control group. But of course the control group doesn't know it. It would be the equivalent of telling a bunch of dysfunctional sociopaths that they were all psychologists and then getting them to diagnose whether the rest of the world was well-adjusted – which is pretty much how the field of psychology came about, come to think of it.

Nowhere do these two worlds collide more violently than in the school system. At the first bell of day one you are trapped in a vast institution where all the children seem to instinctively know how to stratify and divide into their appropriate social order while you of course do not. Everybody is a lot like each other and nobody is anything like you. And yet even this doesn't make you realise that you are weird, it just makes you think everyone else is. The only conclusion is that the whole world is strange and hostile and you are caught in the middle of it, sane and alone.

Needless to say this dystopian conviction was enthusiastically encouraged by my mother, who, despite almost forty years of reluctant interaction with the outside world, was still immovably convinced that it was indeed everyone else on the planet who was crazy and we few Hildebrands the only rational ones. So what if other people had absurd luxuries like new clothes, VCRs or indoor toilets? More fool them.

As the evidence mounted that such absurdities were in fact common to everybody except our family and that the 'other people' were in fact us, my mother gradually changed her positioning to suggest that if indeed they were 'normal' then our family was exceptional, and nobody in it more exceptional than me.

And in a sense she was right. When it came to trying to make friends with other kids it turned out I was, in the most painfully literal sense, the exception. My social quirks, odd personal habits and various eating disorders had no place in civilised society. But rather than these being checked by my mother, they were allowed and sometimes even encouraged to propagate and fester.

This wasn't entirely her fault. When one's closest sibling is severely brain damaged even the most eccentric child can appear quite normal by comparison. Paddy was largely a sweet-natured boy, however it could not be ignored that his favourite hobbies included running away from home, smashing up furniture and attacking people with deadly weapons. When it came to regulating my behaviour, it's fair to say my mother had bigger fish to fry.

This, combined with the obvious economic limitations of a single mother on a pension and a general ignorance of how the rest of society functioned, left our family in a perpetual state that could most succinctly be described as poor, stupid and crazy.

For starters, throughout our whole childhoods none of us had ever worn a new item of clothing nor a haircut acquired at an actual hairdresser's – two factors alone which have been known to cause certain death in the schoolyard. Even simple routines like taking a daily shower or doing the dishes at the end of each night were never quite taught, let alone ingrained, which naturally led to their own social problems.

Indeed anything plumbing related seemed to pose particular challenges at our house, the most confronting being the fact it did not have an indoor toilet. Instead we had an outhouse at the rear end of a dark and spider-infested shed which could only be accessed by walking on razor-sharp gravel while ducking and weaving between the overgrown thorny creepers that hung from the side wall. And even if you did survive the perilous journey your only reward was to sit on a suspiciously sticky seat whose temperature often dropped below zero, surrounded by mosquitos and cobwebs, and with only a single candle by which to peruse the yellowed pages of 1970s self-help books which my mother had been stacking against the walls for as long as I could remember.

The rest of the house was, as might be imagined, in a similar state of chronic untidiness and disrepair both inside and out. My mother was a pathological hoarder and found ever-more inventive ways to create stacks upon stacks, piles upon piles, until the whole interior was effectively just a rabbit warren of pathways dug out among the clutter in order to allow passage between such basic necessities as bed, kitchen, television and door.

This living arrangement meant that social interaction was not only just awkward but often physically impossible. Never seeing much need for strangers at the best of times – 'strangers' being what my mother deemed anyone unrelated to us – even on the rare occasions my overworked and exhausted mother would allow friends to visit there was the very real possibility that they would simply not be able to fit inside the house. Among my brother and sister and I there was already fierce competition for the few accessible sitting locations available. To introduce an extra body into the equation presented an almost unsurpassable logistical dilemma.

Even getting to that point was to assume that I had made a friend to invite over in the first place – no small challenge in itself – and that the friendship could withstand the shock of them seeing the place. And if it did there remained the problem of the toilet, which made many a guest's eyes water under the strain of desperate bladder control. Over the years I had observed more than one girlfriend manage anywhere up to 24 hours in the house without succumbing to nature's urges. Needless to say my own natural urges often went similarly unfulfilled during their stay.

And the social dislocation didn't end at our surroundings. Where other kids had Vegemite toast for breakfast, we had chapattis. Where other kids watched the *A-Team*, we watched the ABC. Instead of chocolate, we had carob. Instead of toys we had books.

But far from seeing all this as a problem my mother saw it as an asset, as though she had deliberately constructed a fortress of chipped vases, three-legged furniture and home-dubbed Nana Mouskouri tapes for the express purpose of warding off unwelcome invaders. There was always a sense – and at times an open decree – that we didn't need outsiders any more than we needed their possessions. Everything we could possibly want was right here. The whole environment was fiercely warm and fiercely loving but it left no room for others, which was exactly how my mother liked it.

In short, my school years were, for want of a better word, complicated.

Take, for example, kindergarten, a perfectly noble government initiative to introduce children to broader society and make their transition to primary school as gradual and painless as possible. Surely such a kind and altruistic notion couldn't possibly cause any harm?

Certainly there was nothing whatsoever wrong with Dandenong Kindergarten. It was a modest collection of rooms set around a generous and leafy play area all of which was hemmed in by a tall wire fence in the middle of Dandenong Park. Like any pre-school it was based upon structure, routine, social interaction and communal activities such as everybody eating the same food, playing the same games and singing the same songs – not to mention sleeping at the same time.

Unfortunately there was not a single aspect of this that didn't fill me with deep existential terror. A regime where I was told not just what to eat or what to do but also whether I could or couldn't be conscious was both foreign and unthinkable. The very concept of order, let alone its practice, was completely unknown to me.

And so while the other kids laughed and frolicked and fought in the playground I would spend every recess sitting on a thick log that ran between two dirt mounds staring longingly at the gate, hoping against all rational cause that my mother would spontaneously appear to save me from this alien world.

Saving Superman

Despite such a promising start, school was still to be something of a challenge for me. My mother arrived at a mid-year parent–teacher interview in Grade Prep and was shocked to discover that I had spent the previous two terms worth of lunchtimes wandering around the oval in circles by myself.

Far from seeing this as a clue that my upbringing had perhaps gone awry, my mother instead denounced it as a systemic failing on the part of Dandenong Primary School and probably some kind of a criminal offence. She whisked me away on the spot and declared that the only possible remedy was for me to be home-schooled.

Clearly my social situation was not heading for a breakthrough any time soon.

In her defence, my mother was in fact a trained teacher, and an excellent one at that. Long before entering school I was reading, writing and drawing at levels far above my age – skills which I exclusively used to compose comic books – and the endless array of aptitude tests I was subjected to all recorded unusually high scores, especially, it seemed, when they were marked by my mother herself. The only thing she couldn't teach me was how to make friends.

After six months of home school, that reality was no longer avoidable. The state required that I re-enter its education system – as opposed to, say, my mother's. While the curriculum didn't express it in quite so many words, it was time to get my goddamn shit together.

Still, the problem of my abject friendlessness remained and so the government found a solution to that too: If I couldn't find a friend myself, the state would appoint one to me.

It says much about the efficacy of government intervention that the child chosen to make me more popular was universally considered the single biggest nerd in school – at least until I came along. His name was Gareth Rees and it's fair to say that our state-sanctioned friendship did little to help either of us climb the social ladder. Nonetheless, at least I had someone to talk to, which was a 100 per cent net improvement on the previous state of affairs.

Gareth seemed unusually enthusiastic about the new arrangements and it soon emerged he had a particular use for me in mind. At the first lunchtime after I was passed into his custody he asked me in a hushed voice if I would like to join his gang. This carried a note of immediate danger to me – the only gangs I had heard of were of the criminal kind routinely defeated by the Justice League of America. Surely this could come to no good?

'What's the name of the gang?' I asked, thinking I might recognise it from one of my comic books and thus be better informed to make a decision.

Gareth's eyes darted from side to side to make sure no prying ears were listening.

'The Mad Scientists Club,' he said.

If there was anything more nerdy than not having any friends at all, it was this.

The club was made up of Gareth, who was obviously the leader, a pale blond boy called Alex, who repeatedly emphasised that he was the second-in-command, and a Sri Lankan kid called Roshan, who single-handedly comprised the rest of the membership. Gareth solemnly informed me that should I meet all the necessary requirements and pass the induction test it was possible there could be an entry-level position available.

The prospect filled me with enormous excitement, although not half as much as it did Roshan, who finally saw his chance for a tilt at the as yet uncreated third-in-command position. Sure enough, soon the Mad Scientists Club had not two but three official office holders and a remaining membership of me.

The purpose of the club was not immediately clear to me. My induction involved us heading to a muddy drain in a far corner of the schoolyard and scooping out gunk until someone discovered a rusty old teaspoon which, as the leader of the expedition, Gareth immediately declared to be his. Other than that the club appeared to involve little more than running hurriedly to inspect various nooks and crannies around the school grounds and repeated affirmations of who the first-, second- and third-in-command were. It was undoubtedly the zenith of my social life so far.

However even the obvious mainstream appeal of the Mad Scientists could not save me from myself, nor my mother's misguided notion that my stubbornly untempered individual 'flair' was something to be encouraged. This new systemic failure came home to roost on a fateful dress-up day when students were invited to come to school in the garb of their favourite book character.

It was another case of the state having the finest of intentions. What better way to make reading fun and encourage children to discover the joys of literature? What, once more, could possibly go wrong?

The answer to that question germinated, as it usually did, in a discussion with my mother, this time about whether Superman was a genuine book character or not. Certainly, I argued, he was a comic book character, and what were comic books if not — as their name suggested — books? Either way it hardly mattered. So determined was I to don the red cape that if push came to shove I would have written a book about him myself.

Naturally my mother wholeheartedly endorsed the idea, and the evening before the dress-up day was spent rummaging through countless overstuffed wardrobes and piles of long-forgotten clothes. It went without saying that purchasing an actual costume from an actual costume shop was completely out of the question.

Eventually a piecemeal ensemble was put together comprising a bright blue girl's leotard, a bright red pair of girl's briefs and some fetching blue stockings that, lest the theme go unnoticed, were also designed for a girl. The linen closet eventually yielded a musty red polyester sheet that made a fine cape which, along with a painstakingly decorated cardboard 'S', was carefully safety-pinned to the leotard centrepiece. Australia's criminal underworld was no doubt already quaking in its boots.

Unbeknownst to them, however, the boots themselves remained the missing piece of the puzzle in their nemesis's outfit. For a moment it seemed the solitary item our house did not contain was a pair of red knee-highs that could equip a five-year-old boy for fighting crime. Then late in the night my mother's ingenuity intervened, as did the 1970s. She managed to find a pair of old tan leather zip-ups and spent several Artline textas colouring them a deep scarlet. When I tried them on they almost came up to my waist and my feet slid back and forth in them like a rowing machine but it didn't matter: I had my Superman boots at last — even if they were ones with slightly higher heels than I'd remembered him wearing.

When I presented at school the next day I could not have been more proud, nor more convinced that the innumerable bullies I had previously encountered would finally realise that here was a force to be reckoned with. Once they saw I was a superhero they would surely not dare continue their campaign of vilification. That much was obvious.

And it must be said the early signs were promising — certainly I at least stood out from the crowd. As it turned out only half the kids in the class had bothered to dress up, and of those who did there were three Robin Hoods, two Sherlock Holmeses and the rest were in plastic Darth Vader masks purchased at the Dandenong Show earlier that month. Gareth had also apparently come dressed as Doctor Who but nobody could tell the difference. Teetering into the classroom in two-inch heels and a festival of elasticised spandex, not to mention the flowing red cape, I soon realised that I had perhaps overcommitted.

It was morning recess that revealed, as it always did, the true state of play. I quickly discovered that the Robins, the Sherlocks and the Darths all had one thing in common, being that they could remove their headgear and instantly go back to looking like ordinary kids – albeit in the case of the Robins, kids who had a particular fondness for green.

My particular choice of outfit did not allow for such anonymity. The Son of Krypton, as I well knew, was one of the few superheroes who was himself in his super form, as opposed to the countless others who donned a mask to perform their extracurricular activities. It was only when he needed to blend in among Earthlings that Superman donned a nondescript suit and glasses to become the mild-mannered Clark Kent. And what I would have given for a pair of horn-rimmed spectacles as I strode out into the playground that day.

Wearing my mother's newly red boots it was hard enough to remain vertical, let alone maintain the kind of bold imposing carriage that befitted the Man of Steel. This much became clear when I literally stumbled across a group of Grade 2 kids whose number, I quickly registered in horror, included the well-known playground menace 'Peter Bannon the Cannon'.

Bannon's arsenal of terror was, as far as anyone knew, bottomless. He was a tall angry kid with thin eyes and thin lips and a wiry frame, all of which gave him the shape and demeanour of a nasty stray cat. He could run fast and punch hard and did both with equal relish. It was whispered within the ranks of the Mad Scientists that even Gareth was scared of him.

Confirming this suspicion, Gareth tip-toed up beside me and whispered, 'I think we'd better go.' In true Mad Scientist fashion, he did this as though the Grade 2'ers were obliviously sleeping in our midst, as distinct from being in the process of surrounding us whilst collecting rocks. Clearly there would be no easy escape nor gallant retreat. The last thing I remember before the barrage began was Bannon shouting, 'Holy shit! He's wearing fuck-me boots!'

The rest of morning recess and the following lunchtime was spent running away from Bannon and his evil horde of followers as they pelted stones at us from what must be said was often unsportsmanlike proximity. By afternoon recess I simply went into hiding, Gareth having found a particularly suitable ditch during his scientific excavations.

After hours of immersion in fear and sweat and mud I survived the day, but Bannon's reign of terror continued for months afterwards. Eventually on one otherwise pleasant afternoon as I was walking home from school he ran up behind me, whipped a sharp blue strip of plastic around my neck and set about strangling me with it. I had little doubt I was departing from the world until my mother, who had whimsically decided to wander up the street to greet her beloved son instead saw him being garrotted by a street urchin.

In a split-second she shot towards us as though she'd been fired from a gun and pounded into Bannon like a runaway train. As the plastic strip fluttered to the ground he staggered back, his nasty narrow eyes now as wide as an animal's caught in the nexus between fight and flight. Behind them I could almost see his psychopathic little brain calculating the options. This was both a grown-up and a woman, he was thinking. No way could she hit him.

But my mother had become an animal too. She barely glanced sideways to check I was still breathing, instead focusing the full force of her flame-rimmed gaze upon the Cannon himself, who was now backed against some unsuspecting homeowner's front hedge. As his eyes flitted she toed the ground like a boxer or an angry bull. There was just enough time to see Bannon's pupils retract and dilate before she lunged forward with a darkened growl: 'Come here you little shit!'

With an impressively deft duck of the head, Bannon slipped out from his corner and bolted down the street and my mother launched after him. He slowed briefly for a second to turn his head only to jump when he saw her reaching for his neck. That was enough to send him to the next level and he flung his legs even further in front of him until he was a speck at the end of the street. For all his legendary speed I had never seen him run as fast as he did that day.

My mother strode back to me with her chest heaving and arms swinging.

'Nearly got him,' she said, as she put her arm on my shoulder and pointed me towards home.

A Good Girl

Still, even superheroes have their flaws.

My mother's strict policy of never buying anything other than secondhand clothes earned me the nickname 'Op Shop Flavour'. The moniker stung all the more because it was bestowed upon me by Roshan, whom I'd not only helped to become third-in-command of the Mad Scientists Club but who was also my new best friend. Primary school breeds fickle allies.

Likewise my mother's vehement opposition to taking me to a professional hairdresser – or possibly just her ignorance that they even existed – had resulted in me having a luxuriant mane of rich, full-bodied locks that would have been the envy of many a Bee Gee. However, there were precious few Bee Gees in Grade 6 that year and my long flowing hair could best be described as either distinctly ahead of its time or distinctly behind it. Either way it certainly did not belong in the present.

This became starkly apparent when the class was treated to a special guest in the form of 'The Mathemagician', a genial older man who was the latest footsoldier in the education department's constant unwinnable struggle to somehow make maths engaging for students. The school had struggled with this endlessly and had eventually come to the conclusion that the only way to make maths fun was to discard mathematics classes altogether.

This was where The Mathemagician – who was, it later turned out, a chorister at St Mary's Catholic Church called George Thompson – came in. With clownish zeal he harried us with a series of silly puzzles that largely involved reading things backwards or turning calculators upside down. For a generation of children who had only just learned how to write the word 'BOOBLESS' on a calculator it was compelling stuff.

Then, according to plan, he surreptitiously crept into the realm of real maths problems in the hope that the kids wouldn't notice. But the appearance of real numbers on the blackboard and nothing being turned upside down immediately set off alarm bells in the class, which is to say every student fell silent and sullen. Just when we were actually getting excited about something it turned out the bastards had been trying to trick us again.

Sadly one sprightly student at the back of the class had failed to pick up on the consensus position. And so when, after scribbling yet another puzzle on the board, an increasingly desperate Mr Thompson looked around and asked if anyone knew the solution, I threw up my hand flush with ill-begotten confidence.

Whether stemming from his love of the church choir or his secret identity as The Mathemagician, Mr Thompson had both a keen sense of showmanship and a knack for filling uncomfortable silences. Knowing this moment might yet make or break his mission to instil numeracy in Dandenong's wayward youth and indeed his prospects of a callback, his twinkling eyes bored deep into my soul and he asked me once more if I was sure I knew what the answer was.

Yes, I declared. And gave it to him.

Sure enough I was right and George Thompson clapped his hands with glee. Suddenly I was part of a breakthrough moment in Dandenong's educational history.

'Good girl!' he said.

In Mr Thompson's defence, it was undeniably true that I had rich and shiny shoulder-length hair, full pink lips and was wearing a colourful turtle-neck skivvy. But just because you look like Joan Baez doesn't mean you deserve to be treated like her. It is a sad enough moment when a young boy is called a girl by his classmates; when he is called a girl by his teacher the situation is, to put it mildly, unrecoverable.

The most extraordinary thing about the whole episode was that even when caught in a perfect storm of humiliation, I still managed to find a way to make things worse. First, having just been called a girl in front of the entire class, my reaction – before I could even think or speak – was to suddenly burst into tears. This response did little to boost my masculine credentials.

This dramatic escalation of embarrassment was as much a shock to me as it was to my classmates, who were now looking at me with the sort of stunned apprehension usually reserved for large recently deceased roadkill. However it was my next move that really took me into new and uncharted heights of self-immolation.

Realising I had to do something dramatic, I threw back my head, put a hand against my brow and exclaimed, 'It's the glamour of it all!' in much the same way that a Hollywood starlet might accept an Academy Award. I reasoned that this would convince everybody that the whole thing had been a carefully planned act orchestrated purely for their entertainment.

Perhaps, predictably, this did not have quite the effect I had hoped for. My classmates went from laughing uproariously to regarding me with confused pity. Up until three minutes ago all they'd had to deal with was a quiet nerdy kid who happened to look like a girl. Now it appeared they had in their midst some kind of schizophrenic eleven-year-old transvestite.

As soon as the final bell rang I took all my bottled-up rage and ran home to vent it upon my unsuspecting mother, whom I told the whole horrible tale in a single heaving breath.

'Oh darling,' she said. 'Don't listen to them. You've got *beautiful* hair.'

The Gentle Art of Dentistry

Say what you like about hair, at least it can be cut. Teeth, on the other hand, are more stubborn enemies.

I was only just recovering my standing in the Dandenong Primary School community when on an otherwise unremarkable Friday morning a large white van suddenly appeared in the schoolyard. Like any new and foreign object it had a magnetic effect on children, who began milling around it with awestruck whispers, as if an alien spacecraft had landed.

When we were finally corralled into class the teacher animatedly told us that we had some very special guests at the school that day, a statement that naturally filled me with dread. I did not have a good track record with special guests.

Our visitors, the teacher went on, had come in a very special van. Would we like to see what was inside it? In a result that will hearten kidnappers across the country, the overwhelming answer was yes.

One by one throughout the day each student was spirited out of the classroom and marched outside by a lady in a white coat. All returned smiling, in the same way that some corpses do after being administered certain poisons. Then it was my turn.

The lady in the white coat appeared at the door and called my name and I dutifully trotted away with her. She led me to the van, opened a door in the side and beckoned me to climb the three steel steps and enter. It was the mid-1980s and every TV show worth watching starred a vehicle possessed of some supernatural powers, be it the talking car in *King Rider*, the jumping car in *The Dukes of Hazzard* or, my personal favourite, the incredible *Transformers*, in which cars and trucks and planes could not only change to robots and back again but also, in the case of Optimus Prime, summon a 60 foot semi-trailer out of thin air. Whatever was inside this van I had no doubt would be the best thing I had ever seen.

But instead of a convoy of Heroic Autobots I was greeted by walls adorned with colourful charts, pictures of smiling kids and various depictions of cartoon toothbrush and toothpaste figures enthusiastically extolling the virtues of dental hygiene with verses such as *Brush your teeth and you'll feel great underneath!*

In the centre was a large mechanical chair adorned with buttons and levers and all kinds of machinery. I sat down in the chair as instructed and marvelled, somewhat nervously, when with the flick of a switch it whirred to life, simultaneously rising up, extending out and reclining back while a light on an attached metal arm swung around above. For a brief moment I allowed myself some remaining hope that it might yet transform into a robot and help me take revenge on Jason Briffa for stealing all my pencils but it soon became clear this was not that day. Instead a kindly older man with a plastered side-part and odd-looking glasses appeared from a corner, peered into my face and bid me open my mouth.

One of the reasons dentists will never truly be accepted into the medical fraternity is that doctors are trained to regard all conditions with calm and detached impassivity. They are supposed to nod their heads imperceptibly and mutter things to themselves such as 'mm-hm' and 'uh-huh' that reassure the patient that everything is completely as expected and there is nothing whatsoever to worry about. What they are not supposed to do, for example, is recoil in horror and use phrases such as 'My God!'

Dentists, on the other hand, suffer under no such restraint. On the contrary they seem to enjoy punctuating their examinations with sharp intakes of breath and decidedly unmedical expressions such as 'Whoa!' Even so, when a dentist audibly gasps at your teeth it is a fair indication you are not destined for a pleasant experience. Explaining my orthodontic situation to my mother, he said the only way he could think to describe what he'd seen was that 'it was like looking at the Himalayas'.

To put it less geologically, the symmetry that defines most dental formations was almost provocatively absent in mine. Of my four front teeth, two were at right angles to each other, which I was now given to understand was not normal. Of my two canines, one was in a perfectly normal position however this only served to draw attention to the fact that the other was protruding from so high up in the gum it looked like it was about to go to war with my nose.

Meanwhile my lower incisors were so closely bunched together it looked like they were in a rugby scrum. Instead of being lined up in a neat little row they had managed to form a sort of crosshatch shape, like a chequerboard.

Not only were my upper and lower jaw both beset by internal revolution, they were also at war with each other. Just to complete the catastrophe, I had a major crossbite, meaning that when I closed my mouth the two sets of molars almost bypassed each other completely, like a game of British bulldogs played by blind people.

Point being, there was another way the dentist might have explained what was wrong with my teeth: Everything.

When I returned to class after my visit to the dental van I could not smile. Not only was I the recipient of unhappy news but, I now realised, to do so would inflict unspeakable aesthetic cruelty upon my fellow human beings.

After receiving the verdict, my mother reacted with great force and alarm, which might seem an odd response given that she of all people must have been aware that my teeth had been like this for some time. This at least vindicated the dental profession's affection for the 'shock and awe' diagnosis. How else could they convince a patient that the smile they thought was perfectly passable was in fact a horror show requiring thousands of dollars worth of treatment?

The problem was we didn't have any money. The dental van was a government-funded service provided for free to schools in the interests of a happier, smilier nation. But while it performed exceptionally well in identifying problems, it had no capacity by which to solve them. That afternoon the dental van retracted its collapsible steel steps, shut the door and moved on to the next primary school in need.

Soon the Victorian public health service was to learn, just as Bannon the Cannon had a few years earlier, that when it came to the protection of her children my mother's clutches could not be escaped so easily. And for someone who had spent her whole life outside of 'the system' my mother had an almost supernatural talent for infiltrating it.

To this end she quickly discovered that while the dental van's only obligation was to provide free dental care to children at the primary school it happened to appear at that day, there was nothing in its charter that specified the child had to come from that particular school.

And so for the rest of that year my mother and I spent the last Friday of every month chasing the dental van around the suburbs of Melbourne. Thanks to a steady campaign of harassment against low-level bureaucrats she had managed to obtain the whole itinerary of its metropolitan pilgrimage. Sometimes her intelligence was so good we ended up tailgating the van to its next destination.

Every few weeks I would be whisked through the gate of a new suburban primary school and presented at the dental van for my next appointment. It had by now become a sort of TARDIS – whatever strange and foreign environment I found myself in, however far from home, I would step inside the door and find the same crew in the same familiar and surprisingly roomy surrounds.

Eventually, either complicit in this scheme or merely worn down, the dentist presented me with a polycarbonate plate affixed with grim wires and one particularly aggressive steel protrusion that was meant to press against my right front tooth at all hours of the day and night, thus forcing it to comply with society's incessant demands for perfection.

The plate was a source of both constant aching pain in my front incisor and constant happiness in my mother. However, despite its best efforts even this hardy little torture device could not defeat my stubborn mouthbones and so I entered high school as dentally deformed as ever.

The Little Engine That Could

From what has been written one could be forgiven for thinking my mother was responsible for every schoolyard torment I suffered as a child. But of course it would be too simplistic and unfair to land the blame for such complex and wide-ranging problems at the feet of one person. To really do the job it takes two.

My father was about as obsessed by my educational future as he was about lawn maintenance, which is to say not particularly. Despite being a Harvard man himself, he felt there was little practical value in a university education. This was possibly due to the fact that he had decided to major in Latin and minor in Ancient Greek and yet still found there was little demand for his skills in the late 20th century job market.

In my early years he offered the sage counsel that 'there's no point going to university if you want to be a musician', which from any other father would have been considered reverse psychology but in his case was meant exactly as it was spoken. When I protested that I wanted to both be a musician *and* go to university he said he supposed that was fine but there was no point going to lectures. Better to just read a book instead or borrow the notes from a friend. Suffice to say, it was not typical parental advice.

But there was one aspect of my education he was zealously insistent upon and no argument about it would be tolerated: As soon as I started high school my first course of action had to be that I would sign up to the choir.

Even in my naïve pre-teen state I suspected that this might not be the key to popularity I had so long struggled to find. It was certainly true that I had dreams of becoming a musician just like my father – albeit a slightly more famous one – however I couldn't help but feel that perhaps my rock star credentials might not be best served by being the only boy in the Dandenong High School choir.

Already things had begun badly. On my first day I announced at roll call that my name was 'John Joseph Hayes Hepburn Broderick Christopher Hildebrand', a ridiculous concoction I had come up with by tallying the names of all my grandparents and throwing in a tribute to Christopher Robin for good measure. I had thought that this might impress my new peers, however it only served to confirm within mere minutes of starting high school that here was a geek of astronomical proportions.

By the end of the first week I had been universally identified as a nerd par excellence – it is extraordinary how fast news of social status travels among adolescents. While wiser nerds than I receded effortlessly into the background, I was a flagship for uncool behaviour. A flaming geek, if you like. Within days the whole school had become little more than a gauntlet of danger zones and more dangerous faces that I had to dodge, ignore or run past just to make it to the next class. The tolling of the final bell always signalled a quiet relief that I had lived through another day – provided of course I could make it to the school gate unscathed.

At the end of one such day I tumbled into the passenger seat of my father's car ready for his regular bi-weekly visitation, which I always looked forward to. This, and the fact I had survived until three-thirty unscathed, put me in an unusually happy mood.

'So,' he said, 'did you join the choir?'

At first I tried to be casually offhand, and talked about how I'd had such a busy week and that with all that had happened I guess I hadn't quite got around to it. However this feigned light-heartedness only made my father turn. With rare forcefulness, he reminded me that it was the one thing he had told me to do and then proceeded to embark on a lengthy soliloquy about how singing in a choir was the best way to learn how harmonies, chord structures and melodic progressions worked together and how his days in the choir at his high school in Colorado had been among the most informative of his life.

It all would have been quite poignant had the whole speech not been delivered in such a menacing tone. To this day I am convinced that this is the angriest anyone has ever become while talking about a glee club.

At the end of it I tried once more to pretend we were having a general discussion about the various options on the table and said I'd certainly look into it. But my father would have none of it.

'Just join the goddamn choir!' he said. It was, again, a sentence I suspect few other fathers have proffered.

Naturally I did as I was told, all the while scrambling around for reasons with which to convince myself it was a good idea. The most powerful argument I could come up with was that with every other member of the choir certain to be a girl, there was at least no chance of me being picked on. Little did I know there was in fact one other boy in the choir and, as he made repeatedly clear, there was room for only one rooster in the henhouse. Next thing I knew I was being bullied by a boy soprano.

At least during this stage any embarrassment caused by my father was limited to school hours. Soon its hours of operation were about to expand.

Usually I would walk the two kilometres to and from school, however on the two nights a week my father came to visit he would, as evidenced by the Choirgate incident, pick me up in the car. At first this was no more than a kindly if possibly lazy gesture – Greg had never had a close relationship with physical exercise – but that was all about to change.

In even the poorest suburb the car is often the last thing to go. A working-class man might lose his job, his house or his family but will hold on to his car for dear life. A man's house might define where he lived; a car defined who he was. At Dandenong High this meant kids were shuttled to and from school in Commodores, Falcons and Corollas. Normal, simple cars for normal, simple people.

My father, on the other hand, was a Moke man.

The Leyland Moke was the proud vehicle of choice for the 1970s hippie, an unusually prized possession for a culture that considered possessions meaningless. In terms of beatnik credit it was rivalled only by the Volkswagen Kombi van – which was his other car. It is probably best described as a cross between an army Jeep and a golf cart.

The Moke had belonged to Joy when my father commenced his affair, and was subsequently welcomed into his fourth marriage as a kind of dowry. In its original state it was an open-shelled vehicle which could be covered with zippered plastic if it rained or if on an awkward date night my father needed to plonk me under a blanket in the back tray while he and Joy rode upfront. (I thought this was tremendous fun and couldn't believe there were other poor kids whose parents forced them to use seats, although it was an arrangement with which my mother was not pleased.)

Along with the Moke, my father seemed to acquire a range of hitherto undiscovered skills in his new marriage. Not only was he now adept at lawnmowing – as my mother noted each time he asked to borrow our mower – but he could apparently recondition cars.

To this end he set about constructing a sheet-metal shell for the Moke which he planned to handpaint himself. For most men this would mean simply applying a primer and finishing it off with a nice gloss enamel but my father had other ideas. This would be his Sistine Chapel, his Abbey Road, an everlasting testament to his love of Joy, his love of music and his greatest passion of all: himself.

The result was a four-wheeled psychedelic shrine that even Wavy Gravy himself might have thought was a bit much. On one side it depicted a wandering minstrel clad in tights and a tunic who slept in a meadow while the notes from his lute floated up to turn into twinkling brightly coloured stars. On the rear it featured two naked cherubs playing trumpets amid white fluffy clouds. On the second side was a group of dwarves whose digging expedition was overseen by an owl sitting on a tree. And lest anyone be in doubt as to who was the owner of this magnificent machine, there emblazoned in giant capital letters were the words 'THE HILDEBRANDS'.

It was this vehicle in which my father collected me from school twice a week. It did not take me long to realise I was going to struggle to blend in.

It's Only Words

For my first two years of high school I was burdened with boofy hair, crooked teeth and a father who ferried me around in what had become known as 'The Hippiemobile'. Still, I was at least comforted by the fact that surely nothing else could possibly go wrong.

It was around this time that I met an athletic young man by the name of Damien Tallis, who introduced himself by walking up to me while I was at my locker one afternoon and punching me in the guts.

I made the mistake of being curious as to who had just belted me and when I turned around to see he responded with the unanswerable question that has echoed from bullies' mouths throughout the ages: 'What are you looking at?'

Unfortunately I answered it. 'You,' I said.

'What are you looking at me for?' Tallis responded.

By now I was really puzzled. 'Because you just hit me,' I said.

Tallis now seemed as confused as I was and so broke the impasse by hitting me again.

'What the fuck did you do that for?' I said. At least my father had taught me how to swear.

'Because you looked at me,' he said.

'I looked at you because you hit me you dickhead,' I said, perhaps unwisely.

'What did you call me?'

'A dickhead.'

Tallis hit me a third time. 'Say it again.'

'Alright,' I said. 'You're a dickhead.'

For some reason this only seemed to upset Damien Tallis even further and he pummelled me a couple of times more before being cajoled away by his ever-present gang of lieutenants, who were perhaps sympathetic to me but more likely just bored.

Meanwhile my own lieutenant Gareth reappeared out of nowhere to offer his own advice.

'You probably shouldn't have called him a dickhead,' he said.

From that day onward Damien Tallis made it his personal duty to deliver as much physical and psychological torment upon me as his large body and small brain could respectively muster, to the point where his daily routine involved walking past my locker at 3.30pm and executing a series of well-practised body blows upon my skinny adolescent torso. Sometimes this was done casually, as though by rote, other times – if perhaps he'd had a bad day at the gym – with somewhat fiercer intent.

My only unwavering policy during each of these encounters was that I always called him a dickhead – even if as I did so I tended to flinch in anticipation of the follow-up punch. I knew, of course, that this meant the beatings would continue both then and there and every day to follow. But it also meant that Damien Tallis would at least go home each afternoon with the declaration that he was a dickhead ringing in his ear. When you have no power – no physical strength, no social clout, no money to buy your way out of trouble – all you have to fight with are words. They are the only weapon of the weak.

When I See You Smile

As befitted my social station in high school I always sat in the front row in class. This was both for instinctively nerdish reasons and also distinctively pragmatic ones. The fact was if I sat any further back I couldn't see the blackboard.

I foolishly happened to mention this to my mother one day and the usual harried wheels were set in motion. It soon emerged that I hadn't been able to see a great deal since birth, it was just that, as with most things, I was too stupid to realise it. It says something for my general disposition that for the fifteen years I had spent on the planet it had never occurred to me that I was extremely short-sighted. Instead I had simply presumed that the world was a blurry place.

Not long afterwards I became the proud owner of a pair of vaguely heart-shaped tortoiseshell glasses that I fancied would elevate me to new heights of sophistication. Unfortunately I took delivery of said glasses on the same day my teeth got smashed in by Damien Tallis on the concrete stairs next to the bike locker, so the overall result was that the first truly accurate image I ever saw of myself was a bespectacled underdeveloped adolescent with a home haircut and half his front teeth knocked out.

This maudlin reflection was being beamed back at me during one of my father's regular visits, thus depriving me of my mother's timely reassurance that I looked as handsome as ever, if not more so. Instead, as I stood contemplating the bold juxtaposition between urbane intellectual and recently bashed meth-head, my father and Joy could only offer that my new look 'added character' in between poorly disguised snickering. Fortunately when my mother finally returned home, at the exact moment I'd been wondering what it would be like to be a lifelong virgin, she did indeed tell me how handsome I was. Then she told me I was getting braces.

My mother had by this time hounded the dental van to its point of origin and thus infiltrated the good graces of the Melbourne Dental Hospital, where apparently – thanks to the fiscal forbearance of the Hawke-Keating government – the children of pensioners were able to receive free treatment. There was therefore no persuading her that for reasons of economic hardship I should just have my shattered front teeth restored without the costly and ongoing expense of steel bands girdered to my mouth. Jesus, I thought. Thanks a lot Labor.

And so from the latter half of Year 9 to the middle of Year 12 I had every tooth in my mouth mounted and bound together by a metal and mortar contraption that looked not unlike the Berlin Wall.

The architect of this gulag was a kindly old professor of orthodontics called Dr Huggins who not only took a keen academic interest in my teeth himself, but also frequently invited his classes to do the same. For the enthusiastic dental students at Melbourne University my mouth constituted a field trip upon which they would marvel at the oral horrors therein.

While I was far from appreciating such good fortune at the time, it turned out that I was in fact fortunate my teeth were as exquisitely horrendous as they were. Instead of being shunted to the back of the queue with some middling affliction, I was a highly sought after case study, a unique combination of blunt force trauma and genetic misfortune. When it came to proving one's mettle in the world of dentistry my mouth was the Holy Grail.

First there was the breakage. Three of my four front teeth had large chunks of bone cracked off them – which, not to labour the point, would not have been possible had they been positioned where they were supposed to be. For two teeth this was simply a matter of putting a cosmetic porcelain cap on them, however my largest front tooth was not about to go so quietly. To execute this task Dr Huggins referred me to a dental surgeon in a distant darkened burrow of the hospital whose location I guessed was chosen so that no one could hear you scream.

Employing the usual steady understatement of his profession, the dental surgeon told me that the nerve had died completely and if it was not extracted the entire tooth would turn black, thus giving me the romantic and employment prospects of a newly released prison inmate. To prevent this from happening he would simply reach up through the newly exposed hole in the centre of the tooth with a serrated steel skewer, hook the dead nerve attached to the inside cavity and yank it out.

Having got my attention, the surgeon further explained, somewhat unnecessarily I thought, that this would put me in a state of unbearably excruciating pain and so he would be administering an anaesthetic. This, he went on, would be delivered by two injections into the gums – however this was not the anaesthetic for the procedure but rather the anaesthetic for the actual anaesthetic, which involved a much larger needle being plunged into the roof of my mouth. Even this, he nonetheless reassured me, would be just a local anaesthetic, and so I would be not only conscious throughout the procedure but also able to see the various sharpened implements entering my mouth followed by a scraping sensation on the inside of my tooth.

If there was such a thing as a merciful God I would have passed out there on the spot. Instead I lay there unable to speak while the dentist methodically made his way through the full catalogue of torture instruments in the order he had promised.

If there is a more terrifying thing than the advancement of a giant loaded syringe towards one's own prised open jaw then I have yet to see it. I also soon discovered that I was not just able to feel the sharpened steel scraping against my inner tooth cavity but also hear it as well. However there is no greater benchmark for a dentist to measure his work against than a child's terror and after an hour and a half of cold-sweated hell the surgical team declared the operation a roaring success.

With the nerve removed and each broken tooth recapped there now remained the much greater mission to unify them as a whole, for which Dr Huggins had prepared his mighty steel contraption. He superglued the girders to my teeth and ratcheted two sets of wires around them, giving them one last crack for good measure before I left.

Every month thereafter I would make the four-hour round trip to Parkville via foot, train and tram and Dr Huggins would cheerfully tut tut my lack of progress to whatever lucky students he had that day, before once more winching my teeth ever closer to perfection.

The braces were intended to last as little as 15 months but sat immovable on my teeth for more than double that. It was not until I was in Year 12 that they were finally removed after countless broken promises of 'just one more month'. By this stage Dr Huggins had long since left the public dental service and it was left to one of his favourite students, a handsome blonde woman with the solidly upper-middle-class American name of Merran Storey, to take pity on my pleading eyes and release me from bondage.

The whole process was so long and arduous that if it had happened in a movie it would have required a montage to rival *Rocky III*. There have been marriages less lengthy than the relationship I had with Dr Huggins and less profound than the one I had with Dr Storey, whom, after she plucked the final brace from my back left molar, I loved more than any woman on Earth.

The Labor government, after more than a decade in power, had granted me the ability to smile again.

The Legend of Jason Stan

My earliest nemesis in high school, although, thanks to Damien Tallis, by no means the worst, was a fellow Year 7 student called Mickey Marsden. Despite us being in the same year level he might as well have come from a different planet. He was remarkably overdeveloped for his age, to the point where he was not only the proud possessor of pimples at a time when most of us eleven- and twelve-year-olds were praying for them but was even starting to get grey hair. This was as sure a sign as any that he had been marked by God to rule us and it was instantly understood that he was unquestionably the coolest kid in school. For all any of us knew he was the coolest kid in the universe.

As befitting that station, and no doubt in part to maintain it – one could not, after all, be top dog without an underdog – Mickey Marsden constantly picked on me: at times pointedly, at times half-heartedly and almost always hilariously. However not once did I begrudge him for it – indeed I would have been surprised if he hadn't. It was as much his pre-ordained duty to tease me as it was my pre-ordained duty to be teased.

Nor was he ever violent, like my more energetic oppressor Brayden King, a particularly psychopathic Year 8 student whom I once had to dislodge with a judo throw onto the concrete quadrangle. Ever after that lucky victory any encounter with young Brayden meant certain death but an encounter with Mickey Marsden just meant certain embarrassment: a one-liner that would make everyone collapse in howling fits of laughter, including, needless to say, Gareth.

Because Marsden wasn't a brutal enforcer – he didn't have to be. He was a king, the king of us all, and so I never resented it and never questioned it. My only thought was how can I *be* it. And then, one day, it all became clear.

The year was 1991 and the atmosphere electric. Nirvana was at the top of the charts and the smell of teen spirit was in the air. The place was junior assembly, an august body of which, being in Year 9, we were the undisputed rulers. Perhaps more important than any of this was that assembly took place in the period just before lunch. The population of Dandenong High School was hungry for sausage rolls and hungry for change.

The headmaster at the time was Bryce Redding, an old-fashioned man who seemed lost in a world in which men didn't wear hats and women were allowed to drive cars. His regular assembly speeches usually alternated between rambling laments about the vandalism of public phone booths and wistful predictions that we would all remember these days as the happiest of our lives, especially when we were called up to fight at Gallipoli. It later emerged that he had been suffering from early onset dementia.

But this day was different. Today Mr Redding promised us something big. We had, he revealed, a very special guest — a prospect I had long realised never ended well. We would soon be witnessing a performance never before seen at a Dandenong High School assembly — a quixotic irony, he explained, because the performer himself was a young man who had attended this very institution. A young man who was the living embodiment of what hard work, ambition and a healthy dose of school spirit could do for one in life.

Our guest, he said, was a world-renowned star of the stage, but knowing that his youthful charges might be skeptical about an old man's knowledge of such things he produced with ruddy-faced pride the final piece of evidence that we were about to receive a true god of the rock and roll pantheon. This young man, he said, had once played support for none other than Richard Marx.

Richard Marx, as all music lovers will be aware, rocketed to international attention with his seminal 1988 hit 'Endless Summer Nights'. After this breakthrough he subsided briefly, only to confound his doubters with the number one single 'Right Here Waiting' from his edgily titled 1991 album *Repeat Offender*.

Even after this tour de force, and lest anyone think he was a flash in the pan, he gave the world the song 'Hazard', an ambitious musical tale of a falsely accused murderer known for the haunting lyric about last seeing a woman by the river — which is also where some of his doubters felt that song should have likewise been laid to rest.

The announcement sent a shockwave of thrill and puzzlement through the crowd of more than 500 students.

The name 'Richard Marx' may not have been scrawled across as many folders as it was a year or two before, but it remained eternal. We were ready for something big.

'And so I present to you,' Mr Redding said, his voice rising like an auctioneer, 'the one, the only, *Jason Stan!*'

There was, in the half-second between his final climactic words and the parting of the curtain behind him, just enough time for a collective draw of breath followed by a stunned and deeply concentrated silence. Thoughts travel quickly between teenagers and there was only one thought that moved amongst us then: *Who the fuck is Jason Stan?*

Our question was soon answered. As the curtains receded as though in shame an improbably pretty young man with a sleeveless T-shirt and flowing honey-brown hair burst forth on the stage and commenced leaping and thrusting about with the happy obliviousness that only singers seem to acquire.

There was only one response any group of self-respecting teenagers could offer to such an entrance. And so we started a riot.

The few teachers who hadn't dozed off during Mr Redding's introduction quickly sniffed the winds of anarchy that were shortly to take hold, but even they were powerless to stop the coming apocalypse. The banks of chairs – cast-iron pews whose long-defaced vinyl seats flapped up as soon as their occupants did – were empty in seconds and effortlessly cast aside. In a more reflective mood Mr Redding may even have admired the teamwork with which his students picked the chairs up and flung them towards the walls and the more somnolent teachers still standing against them.

In the meantime those not hurling furniture rushed to the front of the stage and formed an impromptu mosh pit — is there any other kind? — in which school ties were ripped off for the purpose of becoming either headbands or a means by which to strangle fellow students.

Gauging my own place in this new social order, I decided to avoid the mosh pit but approach the stage from the side, carefully stepping over the downcast chairs and occasional Year 7 corpse. It was from this vantage point that I looked up to discover the identity of Jason Stan's lead guitarist, a lion-maned guy in my music class known primarily as 'Ash the Bogan'. I'd remembered thinking even amid Miss Vrisk's tone-deaf tuition that he was an exceptional guitar player, and he was certainly performing at the height of his talents that day: Every note was in place, every power chord majestic.

By this stage Jason Stan had taken full flight and was leaning over the front of the stage rippling his hand through the crowd like our very own Jon Bon Jovi, still blissfully unaware of the seething monster he was titillating. More worryingly, I saw Ash taking careful note of Jason's rock star moves, and witnessed in slow motion the germination of his own wild idea.

My whole school life had been spent in the careful avoidance of danger. It was the one subject in which I truly excelled. The trick of course was to never be in the same place as the danger and so you had to anticipate it, feel from a distance all its subtle escalations and movements, and then get out of the way. When it came to predicting outbreaks of violence I could have sensed a peacenik dropping a flower during the Summer of Love.

Here in the Dandenong High School hall, with Jason Stan broadcasting yet another self-penned power ballad, I didn't just sense trouble, I felt it gathering force inside my body. The bus crash had already happened and we were all just waiting to fly through the air.

And sure enough, Ash was steadily marching towards it. The only danger he sensed was some other bouffanted show pony stealing his glory. If Jason Stan could do it, he reasoned, then why the hell couldn't he?

Step by step Ash crept towards the edge of the stage, shuffling sideways so as to maintain his vital triangular lead guitarist pose. Then, secure in his footing, he leaned forward to sweep his own hand through the adoring crowd of teens. From that moment he was a dead man.

First, his outstretched hand was seized by every paw it came in contact with and pulled down towards the heaving crowd. Ash was at first elated and then alarmed as his erstwhile fans refused to let go. As he teetered and shuffled to keep his balance another hand shot up above the lip of the stage and grabbed his ankle, yanking his sneakered foot off the floor and into empty space.

His sense of danger came with full force but too late and in the flash of an eye he was sucked into the angry vortex of blue uniforms whose affection he had courted. His final and impressively swift act had been to unfurl his beloved imitation Les Paul from his body and spirit it up to a roadie who'd come running panicked onto the stage. As he sank beneath the abyss his muffled last words were *'Save the guitar! Save the guitar ...'*

With Ash thus dispatched, the mob's attention now turned to the higher prize of Jason Stan himself, who was still swirling on the other side of the stage and only momentarily perplexed by the sudden disappearance of his lead guitarist. Sensing the time was right to take his performance to the next level, he delved into some unseen repository and began pulling out stacks of various coloured fluorescent T-shirts, each of which featured the words 'JASON STAN' in block letters clearly applied with an iron-on transfer. These he then began hurling out into the crowd.

Here at last was Mickey Marsden's time to shine. A rioting mob might be one thing, but a leader who rises above it and turns that mob into an army ... Well, that's a champion.

With a combination of effortless athleticism – he was, naturally, captain of the football team – and the effortless luck that always seems to accompany such gifts, Marsden grabbed one of the flying T-shirts and slipped it over his school jumper. In the next instant he seemed to disappear altogether only to rematerialise at the front of the stage, thus obscuring the increasingly confused young man who had come to entertain us.

With every eyeball in the room fixed upon him like a supermagnet, Marsden paused for a second. Even he knew that this moment was the greatest he could ever live. Whatever lay ahead of him, whatever lay behind – neither great shakes in the sorry old town of Dandenong – at this point in time he was a god. Whatever he did next would be his legacy forever, his last great gift to history.

He looked to the left of the room, along which a relay team of teachers was sprinting to disable him, then looked to the right, along which more teachers were likewise scrambling to the stage steps. Then he looked to the vast centre, throughout which the aching crowd was waiting, just begging, for his final act.

Mickey Marsden bowed his head, raised it to the crowd, flung his arms out and up with fists pointing to the sky, and with the full-throated voice of a war cry, screamed at the top of his lungs: *JASON STAN!!!!!*'

And with that, arms still outstretched, he fell forward Christ-like into the crowd and was spirited away on loving shoulders until he landed in the arms of the Year 9 coordinator and was likewise spirited to Mr Redding's office.

'What happened?' all of us asked when he was finally released back into the general population. 'Did you get in trouble?'

'Nah,' Marsden shrugged, as though it was the easiest thing he'd ever done. 'I just told him that I really really loved Jason Stan.'

Juliet

It was clear to me then that I would never be as cool as Mickey Marsden. But I could at least hope that I might one day be as cool as Ash the Bogan. After all, we already both knew how to get beaten up – all I had to do was find other common points of interest.

It quickly emerged that a good way of bonding with Ash was to smoke a lot of cigarettes and so I soon coughed and spluttered my way up the full socio-economic ladder from Horizon to Longbeach to Peter Jackson until Ash and I found ourselves arguing over whether we were Marlboro Men or Stuyvesant Studs.

In between cigarettes we also found time to share our love of music, even if I was constantly apprehensive that any band we formed would involve Ash playing lead guitar and vocals and me on keyboards and hand-claps. Nonetheless, he was soon my best friend and by the age of sixteen we both agreed that we were hard-living men of the world, having fulfilled all the necessary manly duties of chain-smoking, playing guitar with lots of distortion (or in my case listening to Ash play guitar with lots of distortion) and shagging lots of girls.

The only catch was that when it came to the last bit I hadn't quite upheld my end of the bargain. This isn't to say I didn't have some excellent sex stories – most notably one about an older woman from Canada who inexplicably seduced me on a ski trip – it's just to say that none of them were, if one wanted to apply the strict dictionary definition of the word, true.

Once more I needed a saviour and once more the Good Lord provided. Her name was Kirsty Ann Bunt, which one might have presumed was a joke had she not been born years before the first episode of Jerry Springer, and we were brought together by God.

Along with Ash, I had also made a friend called Karl, who had only just arrived at Dandenong High and thus possessed my favourite quality in a person – namely that they did not know anything about me. Thus presented with a clean canvas I was able to do things like, say, observe that a hot new late-night coffee house was opening in town.

It is difficult to describe just how rare was the prospect of somewhere in Dandenong opening past 5pm, let alone a place that might allow teenagers in. The closest we had previously got to a late-night venue was when the local Safeway started trading until 10pm – and even that was cause for some uproar in the community. Of course there was the recently constructed nightclub complex 'Nu Hotel' however this was the preserve of over 18s only. Besides, its burgeoning reputation as a wellspring of violent crime – *The Dandenong Journal* had already begun keeping a tally of stabbings – was enough to keep even people as cool as Karl and me away.

Yet here we were holding a flyer for a café called 'Cornerstone' that was open 'till late' and promised live music, a great atmosphere and 20 cent tea and coffee. Karl and I both agreed it didn't get more hip than that.

We were therefore both quietly disappointed when, having put on our best denim jackets and scraped our hair into ponytails for a Saturday night on the town, we discovered that Cornerstone was not so much a café as a Christian drop-in centre. It quickly emerged we had missed subtle hints in the publicity material, such as the 't' in Cornerstone being shaped like a crucifix or the fact that its menu had roughly the same prices as a soup kitchen – even in the 1990s twenty cents for a cup of coffee represented an unusual bargain.

But of course neither of us could ever admit to ourselves or each other that we were, to use an unchristian term, fuckwits, and so upon entering what we could now clearly see was a renovated church we both wordlessly agreed to pretend that this was exactly what we'd expected the whole time.

And then she came along.

I was hanging out the side door smoking a cigarette, as cool as one could reasonably be expected to be at a Christian outreach centre, when Kirsty Ann Bunt walked in with a phalanx of friends – which in itself was enough to amaze me. Just one look at her peroxide-blonde hair, child-bearing hips and Kuta Lines windcheater and I knew I had found the one.

Kirsty peeled off from her entourage and asked me for a light. This was, not to exaggerate matters, a world first. Not only had I never had a girl approach me, I had rarely seen one not fleeing in the opposite direction. But, like Karl, Kirsty was a clean slate, a girl who knew nothing of my past or nerdish inner core. All she could see was the cool cigarette-smoking loner wearing a white Bonds T-shirt, a ponytail and a smile.

True love being what it is, I didn't remember much of what we talked about that night but I did remember her telling me she worked at Myer, which for a Dandenong teenager gave her about the same social standing as a Vanderbilt. And so after school the following Monday I found myself standing in Dandenong's Palm Plaza outside the famous department store, eyeballing everyone who went in and out, like a dog with dementia trying to identify its owner.

After two long hours this exercise proved to be as pointless as it was creepy and so I decided that the only sensible thing to do was go to her house. She had, after all, specifically mentioned that she lived next door to the Dandenong Workers Club, just around the corner from my grandparents' house. Why on Earth would she say such a thing if she didn't want me to stand outside that for a few hours as well?

Sadly my grand romantic gesture was undermined by Kirsty's father, who, after almost running me over in the driveway, entered the house, pointed out the window and said to his daughter, 'I don't suppose you know that idiot standing on the footpath?'

Shortly afterwards Kirsty came out and got me and I was taken into her life. And what a grateful dog I was.

* * *

For the first three weeks I bombarded her with the words 'I love you' at the same rate with which other people draw breath. Then came the ballads.

I had already written dozens of songs of varying quality, all of which acutely detailed the conflicted and agonising nature of male–female relationships. However, it had to be said that my lyrical enthusiasm was not matched by experience. It remains one of the great failings of popular music that it never quite discovered a gateway genre between nursery rhymes and love songs. And so my mother, with no small degree of consternation, would discover me sitting at the piano with my eyes closed at the gentle ages of six, seven, eight, nine and ten, howling out endless mournful self-penned compositions about how much I craved a woman's touch.

Needless to say by the time I was sixteen and actually had somebody to love my musical output went through the roof. Many were the declarations of burning soulful passions and much was the use of deep lyrical metaphor. Even in the highly competitive world of balladry, candlelight has rarely been described with such a wide range of adjectives.

Eventually, out of boredom or pity or just a desire for some peace and quiet, Kirsty relented and told me that she loved me back. This was a landmark moment in my psycho-emotional development – nobody but my parents had ever told me they loved me before and, let's face it, being hippies they loved everybody. At last I felt recognised, valued, by the outside world.

More importantly, however, it meant that we were finally allowed to have sex.

I had of course long assured her that when we did eventually 'celebrate our love' it would not be my first time. However I suspect that by the time I had unsuccessfully attempted to apply her fifth and final condom she was beginning to have her doubts, notwithstanding my carefully elaborate backstory. Perhaps the fact that my mysteriously misplaced virginity was taken on a ski trip by an unnamed Canadian woman aroused her suspicions. Even among Dandenong's most well-to-do residents ski trips were few and far between, although they were considerably more common than sightings of Canadians.

A week or so later – although unfortunately for me not during the same sitting – I finally managed to complete the act. I was, at last, a man. Granted, a sixteen-year-old man with a ponytail and braces, but a man nonetheless.

What followed was a romance of Shakespearean proportions that I felt sure the great poets would sing of throughout the ages to come. True, I was not a great student of Shakespeare, but I had determined that our song would be Dire Straits' 'Romeo and Juliet', and having listened to it several hundred times throughout our courtship I felt I pretty much had the gist of what the Bard was on about.

Kirsty, on the other hand, had decided that our song would be Meatloaf's 'Two out of Three Ain't Bad', which was, in retrospect, an ominous sign. Still, what could it matter: We were young and in love and with me now in Year 11 and her having just dropped out of school, we had the world at our feet.

Our only problem was one of logistics. While we would spend every single waking hour with each other after school – or in her case just after the otherwise unremarkable time of 3.30pm – talking excitedly about life, the universe and how much she missed her ex-boyfriend Mike, once we had started actually doing it, it was clear we would need a new regime.

And so despite a lifetime of refusing to go to bed under any sufferance, I started feigning early onset tiredness and would declare I was retiring for the evening at increasingly implausible hours. Prior to Kirsty coming along I would be up until 2am every night watching television, reading comic books or, latterly, pulling bongs. But now, as I earnestly explained to my mother, I suddenly felt inexplicably fatigued whenever the clock struck ten.

At first my mother was much relieved that finally some sense of routine had arisen within me, and bade me sweet dreams as I scurried off to my bedroom. Thereupon I would lock the door, slip out the window and trot merrily in the direction of Kirsty's house barely half a kilometre away. Once in the vicinity I would climb over the fence at the Dandenong Workers Club and wait momentarily outside her window until the appointed time.

This was one, possibly the only one, of the many games of infatuation we played. She would ask me to come to her at, say, 10.37pm and I would time my visit so as to appear at just that very minute. The high romance of this was only slightly compromised by the fact that her parents' rather swish modern house had the fiddly roll-out windows that required one to rotate a little handle countless times in order to make the frame tilt out diagonally to expose a gap of a few inches at the bottom. And so rather than appearing Romeo-esque on her balcony, I instead had to perform a tortured calisthenics routine during which my large box-shaped head invariably got stuck between the pane and the ledge and the rest of my body had to be dragged through by Kirsty's burly yet feminine arms.

Once I was safely in, accompanied by only minor scrapes and bruises, Kirsty would beckon me under the covers and we would have more real grown-up conversations about life, the universe, the latest song I'd written for her and of course her ex-boyfriend Mike. Such were the things we had in common that this could sometimes go on for whole minutes until we got around to having sex. Then when that was done she would rest upon my shoulder and ask me to stay until she was asleep, while I murmured sweet nothings and thought up more lyrics about candles.

After waiting an eternity for her to get to sleep – woe betide me if I tried to leave before she had fully gone under – I would carefully extricate myself and somehow manage to eject my body via the downward slot in the window and begin my journey home, there to crawl into bed typically somewhere around 3am. Four hours later my mother would rouse me for the long school day ahead with a pump-action water pistol she kept specifically for such a purpose.

My mother had great faith in the water pistol, and rightly so: It had always done its duty. But when, after a few weeks of my new lifestyle, even a blasting jet of cold water failed to get me out of bed she began to gather her suspicions. Soon we were engaged in a high-stakes battle of wits that escalated into full-blown guerrilla warfare.

First she disabled the lock on my bedroom door so she was still able to check on me after I'd supposedly gone to bed. In response I decided to foil her by placing a series of pillows under my doona with a pair of my sneakers sticking out at the bottom – an ingenious ruse that no parent could crack. Yet she somehow divined that the headless lump who'd gone to bed with his shoes on was not her son, and so she nailed the frame of my bedroom window to the wall leaving only a fixed gap of some nine inches. Again, I could best her. Little did she know that after five weeks of sliding through Kirsty's roll-out window I could've slipped through a crack in a windscreen.

And so I managed to continue my nightly liaisons with the girl of my dreams. Indeed my acts of daring became bolder and bolder until in one especially Oscar-worthy performance I feigned tiredness at 9pm and escaped to meet Kirsty after her waitressing shift at Sizzler, which was at that time Dandenong's fanciest restaurant.

This set a new highwater mark for my clandestine operations but it was worth it. The Sizzler rendezvous were always the most precious to me, representing as they did the closest I had ever come to taking a girl out to dinner. I would wait by the skip bins in the carpark and Kirsty would eventually appear resplendent in her black and white waitressing outfit and, if I was lucky, present me with a half-eaten steak wrapped in a napkin. Of course I would be too overwhelmed by her presence to eat it on the spot but would slip it in my jacket pocket as a treasured token of her affection.

Unfortunately these meaty symbols of love were not as tenderly removed from my pockets as they were placed inside them, as the smell in my room would later testify. And it was this carelessness that led to my undoing.

I was walking hand in hand with Kirsty past the deserted factory warehouses of Plunket Road when I felt the sensation of being kerb-crawled by a suspiciously familiar white Mazda van. From somewhere deep inside it came a voice that was steady with cold measured fury.

'Get in,' my mother said.

The Heartbreak Kid

After three blissful months of fumbling sex, nothing in common and a series of escalating maternal interventions, Kirsty inexplicably dumped me. To my absolute shock it emerged she was still in love with her ex-boyfriend Mike.

After shock, as we all know, comes trauma. And if there was anything my teenage years had conditioned me for it was that. Trauma was my speciality. I could turn anguish into an artform.

For the first five days I refused to shower or change my clothes. Then for three weeks I locked myself in my room smoking cigarettes and listening to country music accompanied only, as you may have guessed, by a candle. To mark my self-imposed incarceration I carved into my bedroom windowsill – which had once been a portal to a better and certainly more sexually active world – the slightly premature epitaph: *'THREE WEEKS – I'M DYING!!!!'*

Then for a week I ran away from home, then for a few weeks more I begged sobbingly for her to come back, then I dropped out of school for six months. All things considered, I thought, I had taken it rather well.

By the end of the year the worst was over. To the great relief of my mother I had returned from Uncle Johnny's St Kilda flat — as runaway attempts went it was a rather lame effort — and to the relief of my few remaining friends I had started showering again. I felt ready to re-enter society and, being a Friday night, this naturally meant going to the Cornerstone coffee house.

I was walking down one of Dandenong's many dark and foreboding main streets, when I saw a group of Kirsty's friends walking towards me and calling out. I had of course come to know them well during our brief relationship so I stopped and waved back. Having acquired over the past year or two not just friends but an actual girlfriend I had presumed that I had crossed over into a world free from imminent threats. In fact the world was more dangerous than ever.

Before I knew it I was pinned against the bluestone wall of Dandenong Town Hall with one of the more squat members of the group — why were the short ones always the angriest? — pressing his arm against my throat and threatening to reconfigure my face with a baseball bat. My only temporary hope was that he didn't appear to have the bat on him at the time, however this comfort was to be shortlived. The others around him were so loudly encouraging this rather Americanised style of homicide that I wondered if they might dispatch a runner to the nearest sports store.

Mercifully, in the midst of the group, there stood a tall, athletic blond man with the sort of square well-proportioned face that inspires confidence and trust. As the pack closed in for the kill he shouted with authority, 'No! Let him go.'

But just as I was thanking as many gods as I could think of it emerged that my noble protector hadn't quite finished his sentence.

'This,' he went on, 'is between him and me.'

Ever astute, it finally occurred to me that the beefy wall of muscle I had been expecting to rush to my aid was in fact Kirsty's ex-boyfriend Mike, whom I now recalled her mentioning had spent quite a bit of time in the Army Reserves. He was not just two years older than me but three times bigger. I had friends who were smaller than his biceps.

Even so I did some quick calculations and realised I'd have a higher chance of survival fighting him one on one than fighting the entire gang – which, presumably, he would be a rather enthusiastic member of anyway. And so I turned my attention back to the howling adolescents around him.

'That's right,' I squeaked. 'This is between him and me.'

For a few moments everything descended into a sort of confused stillness, as Mike waited to see if his band of drunken soldiers would follow his order and the small simian fellow with the baseball obsession complained that he had really been looking forward to bashing me.

Then a small voice from the back of the throng piped up: 'Mike!' it said. *'Stop!'*

And there, after so many months and so many lifetimes of suffering, I once more laid eyes on Kirsty Ann Bunt. Her peroxide-yellow hair had devolved back to its natural mousy brown and her eyes were black and wide and wild, like a frightened deer. Amid her panicked efforts to stop the onslaught she managed to shoot me a look with them that could only be described as urgent regret, as it became increasingly likely she was going to watch me die. Yet even so I found her presence comforting.

At least now, I thought to myself, she'll *really* be sorry.

What troubled Kirsty was that she had told Mike I had snuck into her bedroom. This was, as has been documented, completely and repeatedly true – even if she had not mentioned I had done so purely under her instruction. However what she had also said, as I was gathering from Mike's staccato yet rather emotional interjections, was that I had snuck into her bedroom after the break-up at a time when she wasn't there. This, it struck me, defied the whole point of the exercise. And it was completely untrue. Not only was I still several degrees of separation away from that level of creepiness, I was, on the date of the alleged incident, holed up in my uncle's flat with a packet of Marlboros listening to Elton John sing 'I Guess That's Why They Call It The Blues'.

There were only two people in the world who knew for certain that this was a complete fabrication. One of them was Kirsty and the other was about to get his head kicked in. And it was that knowledge that made her cervine eyes well with fear. As she flashed me her most remorseful 'sorry I got you killed' look, the mass of angry bodies in front of me broke like a wave and lurched forward to tear me apart. If there is anything I have learned in life it is that small lies have big consequences.

Then, out of nowhere, two pairs of lean bare arms reached across and through the mob and broke it apart like a baked potato. Standing in front of me were two men with identical coiffed hairdos, identical white singlets and identically high-cheekboned faces. As I dared to hope I might yet survive and prayed that the small trickle running down my leg was any liquid other than the one I feared, I couldn't help but notice they both looked exactly like Dylan from *90210*.

Having dispersed the mob with lackadaisical ease, the two Dylans asked if I was alright, to which I coolly replied of course I was – as though surprised they even needed to ask. Oh, you mean *that* bloodthirsty mob? I had it all covered until you guys showed up ...

Even so they dutifully escorted me up the street in the direction I was heading, generously disregarding my newly emboldened protests that I wanted to stay and sort things out.

'So what was all that about?' one of them asked as we walked up the hill.

'Well ...' I said, and told them the whole story.

As it turned out the Dylans were bouncers who had run down from the Nu Hotel, at whose doors we had now come to a halt. Once there, they did not invite me in – if the braces didn't violate the dress code then the ponytail surely did – but rather directed me to their car parked on the street out the front. One of them hopped into the passenger seat, flipped down the glove box and let slide out what even my innocent eyes recognised as a handgun.

'If you really want to sort things out,' he said. 'You're going to need this.'

I should have been gobsmacked. Any normal teenager from Dandenong would have either taken the gun and shot the baseball-loving hobbit's nuts off or at least been shocked into a respectful silence. But I was not a real teenager, I barely even lived in the real world.

And so when the Dylan held out the gun in his oddly delicate hand I didn't bat an eyelid – it was the most normal thing in the world. If you were trapped in the desert the army came to rescue you, if your grandma got done for drug dealing the cops would let her off and if you were about to get the shit kicked out of you by your ex-girlfriend's ex-boyfriend and his mob of drunken mates then it only stood to reason that two singlet-wearing martial arts experts who looked like TV stars would save you at the last minute.

'No, thanks,' I said. 'I'll be fine.'

PART II

The People's Hero

Universe City

Throughout the whole bruising obstacle course of my high school years, one thought kept me going: One day I would escape. All I needed to do was keep ducking and dodging long enough to stay alive and then climb up the tangled rope ladder at the end.

But a funny thing happened along the way. No one at school had known who Kirsty was but the fact that I'd managed to get a girlfriend at all had stunned enough people to elevate me one frayed rung above the ground. And the fact that in the throes of heartbreak I had so casually abandoned my hometown raised me a couple more. The coolest thing a student at Dandenong High could do was to leave it – to leave home at the same time was an act of almost divine refrigeration.

It also transpired that after years of studiously avoiding enemies and strategically making allies, I had slowly gathered a circle of friends which ended up settling in the ambiguous layer just beneath the pantheon of high school demigods, still led, as always, by the indefatigable Mickey Marsden – who himself now regularly marked the high point of my day by saying hello to me in the corridor.

In short, I had for the first time in my life achieved the once unthinkably ambitious goal of not being hated.

Meanwhile my braces had at last been removed and my ponytail had finally been stretched into submission. I had a broken heart, powerful hair and a blossoming love of bong-smoking. If this wasn't enough to qualify me for an arts degree I didn't know what was.

These days the academic standards required for an arts degree at a major university are so high as to defy the whole purpose of an arts degree in the first place, which is to provide a place for people who can't meet academic standards. But this was the mid-1990s, a more civilised age when the world was fair and reasonable and people thought the pinnacle of human achievement was the spellcheck button on Microsoft Word.

And so I was accepted into Melbourne University, an improbably august institution for a student of my talents. Yet even in this generous era I was surprised to discover that none of my newfound friends was coming with me. Most hadn't made the university cut and the few that did ended up at more far-flung campuses. My close friend Sally, possibly the smartest girl I'd met at school, faced a daily journey of six hours on public transport to get from Hampton Park to La Trobe University and back. Last I heard, which was twenty years ago, she was planning to give it all up to become a bank teller.

Less progressive social analysts might argue that if more of my friends from Dandenong High had studied harder or perhaps even studied at all then they might well have joined me on Melbourne's leafy bluestone grounds. However, I knew there were more sinister forces at work. As any enlightened intellectual could tell, they were being deliberately excluded from the hegemony by a neo-capitalist class structure designed to oppress the proletariat.

In fact it was vital that none of them did get in, or at least that I believed as much. Otherwise I might have made the mistake of not becoming a revolutionary socialist. Indeed, when I eventually discovered that several of Dandenong High School's nerdier alumni had also got into Melbourne I was first alarmed that they had breached my newfound utopia and then quickly appalled that they had abandoned their working-class roots. On one occasion I even spotted Gareth wandering around the grounds as if he owned the place. 'Well,' I thought to myself, 'there goes the neighbourhood.'

Notwithstanding such interlopers, I remained unshakably convinced that I was the only kid to escape from the badlands of the outer suburbs into the warm bosom of civilisation, albeit a civilisation I was plotting to tear asunder. *I* was the one who had conquered all manner of adversity to get here. *I* was the one who had dreamed this dream of wine-soaked soirees and philosophical debates about the fundamentals of existence. This was *my* secret place, *my* escape plan. As far as I was concerned Dandenong no longer existed.

And so from the moment I set foot on its earth Melbourne University thrilled and entranced me and the more I felt rejected by it the more it absorbed me. Bubbling pools of youths spilled outside the registration hall, glowing in the February sun as though it had been placed in the sky just for them. Clusters of beautiful people migrated from table to table and room to room and pub to pub like a butterfly flitting between flowers. I had stumbled onto the foothills of a new Olympus.

At the same time there was work to do. The recently elected Liberal premier Jeff Kennett had declared war on the noble worker by bulldozing schools, building casinos and closing hospital beds. And when I arrived at university I found out he was trying to introduce something called Voluntary Student Unionism. I didn't know what that was but it sounded like something I ought to be opposed to. For the truly dedicated socialist anything voluntary could only mean trouble.

Along with my thousands of fellow first years, I had been greeted on day one by an address from student union president Rebecca Peniston-Bird, whose closing piece of advice to new students was: 'Love many, trust few, paddle your own canoe.'

It was well metered and it rhymed and she seemed nice enough to me, however I was soon informed by subversive elements in the student body that the fact she didn't call for the overthrow of the capitalist-patriarchal hegemony clearly identified her as a Young Liberal. I struggled to believe it at the time. Surely there was no such thing as a non-left-wing student?

As it turned out this was the first of many things I did not know about student politics. The year I arrived at Melbourne University the union had been taken over by an unlikely coalition of Liberals and the left. The reason for this was that the previous Labor Right administration had been what the journalist in me could only describe as 'engulfed in scandal'.

The word was that this corruption peaked at the purchase of some office couches later transferred to a share house under suspicious circumstances and the mysterious disappearance of a stereo which may or may not have had a five-CD stacker. The most sophisticated extent of their nefarious activity was rumoured to be that the operators of a Chinese restaurant on the ground floor of Union House had been leased this prime location for only a dollar a month. As always the Labor Right's love of Chinese food was their one uncompromising principle.

The hard left were outraged by the administration's bare-faced power grab and the Liberals were outraged by their fiscal imprudence. And so the two extremes, united by both a common cause and a common lack of numbers, combined to oust the dodgy centrists and enter into a somewhat ungodly power-sharing arrangement by which the office bearers would be divided equally between them. Thus the Tory Ms Peniston-Bird got the role of president while some immemorable lefty took the role of general secretary, a position whose title was obviously irresistible to anyone of a communist persuasion.

The marriage – cynics may recoil in shock – was not a happy one, but it gave the hard left its first real taste of power among a traditionally conservative student electorate. And, more importantly, it taught them that if they stopped getting quagmired in angry debates about the merits of Marxism versus Leninism versus Trotskyism versus Stalinism versus Marxist feminism versus feminist Marxism they might actually have a chance of getting people to vote for them.

The key to their success was a small unit of hubristic young turks from the Labor Left who remain to this day the best political operators I have ever seen. Surrounded by Greenies and socialists, the Labor Left kids suddenly found themselves the pragmatic right wing of the newly formed party. This was dubbed 'Left Focus', which was as much a directive to its bonghead membership to get their shit together – as in 'Left: Focus!' – as it was a new political brand. In both senses, however, it was a roaring success. The name was catchy and the effect that the Labor kids had on the aimlessly swirling protest junkies was akin to Graham Richardson running the numbers for an Amazonian hill tribe.

While the rest of the group bickered about ideologies that existed only in leather-bound manifestos, this unofficial leadership group – naturally, being a non-hierarchical organisation, there was no official leadership group – knew of something far more effective than nationalising the economy or redistributing wealth. They knew how to win.

They had memorised every rule and regulation relating to elections, executive office holders, party budgets, union resources and Student Council procedure. They knew how to exploit them, bend them and, when necessary for the greater good, break them. All for the twin goals of glorious revolution and free beer after protest marches, or at least we dumber socialists thought.

The brilliance of this unit was that it was not a standing committee of political strategists – which Sir Humphrey Appleby would call 'a courageous decision' in a party where committees were attributed semi-divine status – but a linear system of acquiring, maintaining and bestowing power.

This last part was critical. Under the union rules no one could hold the same executive post for more than a year and so official power was fleeting. The important thing was not just to win one's station but to make sure the next guy you picked would win after you. The necessary formula was therefore not a fixed body of oligarchs but a master-apprentice style structure, not unlike that employed by the Sith Lords in *Star Wars*.

The master of this apparatus was Danny Bertossa, who at 21 was already an elder statesman in the student community and embodied the finest Labor traditions of pragmatism, cunning and shagging young true believers at any opportunity. He also bore an uncanny physical resemblance to my father. Naturally, I adored him instantly.

When it came to politics Danny was a patient and practical man. After a march against upfront fees, at which a Trotskyite seized the microphone and started braying against American involvement in the Middle East, I had argued that protests against specific causes were too often hijacked and undermined by sectarian elements trying to push their own agenda. They'd be lucky, I said, to get even one out of ten protesters to sign their petition. Meanwhile the other 90 per cent would forget what they'd come to support, thus distracting from our noble cause.

Danny nodded understandingly for a time and said he couldn't agree more. But he also noted that while a thousand people at the protest may have been annoyed, the recruiter from the minuscule Soviet Socialist Workers Society or whatever it was had just signed up ten and might have grown his power base by 50 per cent. When it came to the numbers the Soviet had won. And in politics, Danny reminded me, numbers were everything.

Under such wise tutelage it was perhaps not surprising that the enlightened progressive forces blitzkrieged that year's elections. For the first time in as long as anyone could remember – which given the cannabis intake of its members was about fifteen minutes – Left Focus ruled the union in its own right. A happy year of weekly protest marches, interminable pub debates and fornicating with comrades was sure to follow. The revolution had come early, and the people rejoiced.

Big Red

But even in those heady days politics was not my only passion.

I was stuck in a lift lumbering slowly under the weight of a dozen chattering eighteen-year-olds as we all made our way to sign up for classes in what was by now a conspicuously tall building. As chains of bodies rustled in and out and we eventually crept towards the top I realised I had spent the entire time staring at her face.

In profile it was like a medieval fresco with small perfectly formed features that seemed delicately painted by a grandmaster's hand. But when she turned, her face contorted into new shapes, like one of those old 3D stickers whose image changed as you tilted it in the light. Suddenly it seemed awkward and fragile and disconnected from itself, as though none of the features belonged to each other.

I didn't know if she was just weird-looking or the most beautiful thing in the world. I still didn't know when the lift doors opened and I unthinkingly chased after her. I still don't know now.

Her name was Catherine. She was tall, she was a redhead, she was rich and she was crazy. I followed her at a safe distance on the top floor of the John Medley Building and made sure to sign up to every subject she did. And after finding me sitting improbably close to her in an improbably large percentage of her classes she figured she might as well become friends with me. Then one day our friendship moved into the outside world, where classes and campuses could not contain us.

I was standing at Flinders Street Station, which for any kid from the outer suburbs was both the gateway to the mighty city and a destination in itself. Flinders Street was where everybody met, a teenage town hall. Every day on the steps beneath its grand mustard dome and regal clocks was a waiting guard of wagging students and street kids, buskers and beggars and bright-eyed backpackers who all sat waiting for someone or something to come along and change their lives in one small way or another.

There I was, under the clocks, waiting for nothing and nobody in particular when Catherine's ever-shifting face, unmissable even in a sea of faces, cleaved through the crowd like a ship's prow.

I stood there lurking like an iceberg until she was just metres away, then feet, then inches, then right up against my cheek, which she kissed lightly but tenderly as her arms folded around me. I felt like the 5.17 to St Albans had just derailed through my brain. Before I was able to think, before I even wanted to, I was rushed far away to a perfect place. This, I marvelled, was what Heaven was like. No clouds, no choirs, just the sudden and unexpected moment when two souls align in perfect union.

It was only after the red stains on my cheek had faded that I realised we were not alone. The whole scene had taken place in front of the most terrifying thing I could ever imagine being associated with Catherine: a man.

The first thing I noticed was that he was considerably taller than her, which meant that he was considerably taller than me. In one of many efforts to prove my compatibility with Catherine I had always insisted that she and I were exactly the same height, yet here he was making a mockery of both of us. Plus he had longer hair, which was as aggressive a challenge as one could throw down to another man in the mid-1990s.

And of course he was also absurdly good-looking, bearing an uncanny resemblance to Evan Dando from the Lemonheads – whom, I now recalled, Catherine had repeatedly gone on the record declaring to be her ultimate sexual partner.

'Joe,' said Catherine, 'I want you to meet my boyfriend, James.'

At that moment I saw with absolute clarity that I had to do what any real man would do when fighting for the woman he loved. In many ways I had no choice. And so I pretended I was late for something and ran away after a passing tram.

For days afterwards I wrestled with my heart and my conscience about the right course of action. After long tortured nights of soul-searching I decided I had been wrong to openly pursue Catherine's affections at all costs and at last understood the most important thing was our friendship. All I had to do was figure out how to manipulate it into making her love me.

Palmerston Street

To this end, and for the only time in anyone in my family's life, I had real estate on my side. I was living in a share house in Palmerston Street, Carlton, a block away from campus, with a 30-year-old dope dealer, his psychotic secretary girlfriend, an alcoholic and a speed freak from Adelaide – who happened to be going out with each other – my new best friend Liv, who had sampled all of the above, counting both substances and people, and her friend Joanne, whom Liv had also sampled. There was also a lesbian flautist called Jade – and yes, before you ask, Liv had shagged her too.

I had met Liv and Jo on my first day at uni. Jo had spotted my straggling frame on a campus tour and run up to remind me that we'd been childhood friends. In truth it was our mothers who had been childhood friends and our own relationship had chiefly been defined by my mother telling me how much better at school Jo was doing than me. However, it soon emerged her mother had been telling her exactly the same thing. As we excitedly pulled back the blanket on this great parental cover-up the tour group moved on and we were left to establish a group of our own.

There are moments in history at which the entire future of the world rests on a coin toss. Had the Romans lost Adrianople we might all be Muslim; had the British fallen prey to the Spanish Armada we might all be using pesos; had the Nazis won Stalingrad it is unlikely many of my favourite Woody Allen films would have come to be made.

And had Jo not come up and said hello that day my life might well have been unrecognisable to me today. From one wholly unremarkable chance encounter my planetary passage was redirected. A butterfly had flapped its wings.

That afternoon Jo introduced me to Liv, whose abiding philosophy was that there was no need to worry about childhood competition, nor indeed anything ever, as long as one was perpetually loaded on whatever drug one could get one's hands on at any given time. As a result the three of us ended up that night in a Brunswick supermarket peaking on acid and attempting to eat a trolleyful of lettuce. As the floor manager shouted protests from the other end of the aisle the three of us looked up at each other with leaves hanging out of our mouths and knew that we belonged together.

As fate would have it, fate seeming to favour impoverished drug-addled students, the next day we came across the address '230 Palmerston Street' on a noticeboard at the Student Housing Service, an agency that remains the best advertisement for socialism I have ever encountered.

Back then Melbourne University had a generous stock of terrace houses that it let out to students at an unbelievably low cost so that they might fulfil their undergraduate dreams of societal upheaval and substance abuse – or at least so I took the offer to mean at the time. Palmerston Street was a seven bedroom terrace on the state-sponsored market for $270 a week – about $100 less than one could expect to pay nowadays for a car space in Sydney.

Naturally we deemed this price outrageously expensive, however after some difficult arithmetic, maths never having been an arts student's natural strength, we calculated we could just get by with eight housemates – if you counted Rick's bitch girlfriend.

Finding a group of total strangers willing to cohabitate with each other indefinitely is, for most people, the hardest thing in the world. As any adult knows, the slightest imbalance in a household is a sure recipe for complete psychological breakdown. But for a bunch of newly liberated teenagers in the last decade of the 20th century there was nothing easier than finding a group of people who wanted to live together – especially when there were Austudy payments involved.

The very concept of the share house has an irresistible gravitational pull. It is the temple to which every self-respecting student must eventually come to worship. For one thing it holds the prospect of unimpeded drinking and dope-smoking and for another, not entirely unrelated thing, the prospect of boundless opportunities for clumsy fornication. A good share house sells – or rather rents – itself.

Two days later Liv, Jo and I had managed to recruit Jade the Lesbian flautist, David and Lana, the sophisticated Adelaidean couple, and their dealer friend Rick, whose overseas girlfriend would ominously make up the eight on her return. Rick, David and Lana were all several years older than us and had been flatmates before, having house-sat a heritage-listed mansion in the botanical gardens. There, they said, the preferred method of washing dishes was to hurl them from the upper windows but they assured us this practice was later abandoned due to fears it was drawing attention to the dope crop on the roof. Their credentials thus proven, it was simply a matter of moving in.

But more important than the house's attractiveness to me was its attractiveness to Catherine. As she was still living with her parents, the romance of the share house – or perhaps the fact it was located a mere 150 metres from campus – beguiled her. She would frequently stop into our bong and booze infused oasis on the way back from class before retreating to the comfort of her parents' large and leafy home in the exclusive eastern suburb of Ivanhoe, having cheerfully ignored all my constant pleas to stay.

And when Catherine did at last sleep over it was not as I had imagined, the decision having been dictated by her passing out drunk in Jo's bed and throwing up all over the floor. Of course I considered this simply more evidence of our celestial connection and lovingly cleaned up the vomit, but it was not the romantic breakthrough I had hoped for. Nor did it particularly improve her relationship with Jo.

Despite this setback, I felt sure that having proved myself devoted to Catherine's every need and gastrological expulsion, I would no doubt be more desirable to her than ever. And on one rainswept afternoon at the pub, during one of the many post-tutorial drinking sessions I regularly forced her into, she finally uttered the five most beautiful words in the English language: 'I've broken up with James.'

My face started to spider out into a mottled red in the same way a bottle of wine might if you smashed it on rough concrete.

'We should go,' I said. It was the first time I had ever uttered this phrase in a pub.

I grabbed her hand and dragged her out of the hotel, making a bee line for home – the handy thing about Catherine was that she always seemed to welcome sudden distraction. But unfortunately my charted course took us back through campus, where, one coiffed head at a time, we ended up being trailed by an army of chattering girlfriends wondering where on Earth she could be going with that strange puffing man. Soon the whole mission resembled a scene from *The Benny Hill Show*, only considerably less sophisticated.

It was clear the moment was in danger of being lost. I needed protection, some kind of force-field that would repel all other life forms far from our presence. My mind staggered in a panic through blurry thoughts until it struck me. I had that weapon. I had carried it inside me all along never knowing its true purpose yet I had been doing it my whole life. There was only one surefire way to get rid of girls: All I had to do was play them a song.

I veered left at the Law quad and set a course for Union House, where I knew there was a perpetually disused meeting room with an upright piano stuck against the wall. The squadron of girls fell into formation and soon I was herding them all in, inviting them to a very special musical soiree. Then I sat down at the keyboard.

'This song,' I said, 'is called "Ivanhoe Working Class Hero".'

The crowd started to disperse mere seconds after I struck the first chord, until by the last ringing note Catherine was sitting there alone and unusually still. After a moment she got up and kissed me on the lips, then slowly recoiled in confusion.

'Hang on,' she said, 'I thought we were going back to your place?'

And so we spent the rest of the night back at Palmerston Street, with Catherine's restless weight squiggling on my lap like the small child she wasn't and my housemates slumped in various formations around the lounge room. My world was complete and my happiness electric.

As the clock hands crept together for midnight she peeled herself off to leave.

'I can't be with you right now,' she said at the door.

'I understand,' I said gently. 'I'll see you tomorrow.'

'No,' she said, 'I mean I can't *be* with you right now.'

'That's okay,' I replied, just as gently but somewhat more confused. 'I'm happy to wait.'

'Er, I don't mean *that*,' Catherine said, 'I mean kind of generally.'

All at once the whole night's quota of booze and dope rushed up and enveloped my brain as though it was trying to suffocate it in a plastic bag. 'But …' I stammered, 'we belong together. We're meant to be with each other forever.'

'Yeah, I know,' she sighed. 'That's the problem.'

'How the hell is that a problem?' I sputtered. It felt good to argue with her. At least when I was arguing with her I had a chance.

Catherine rolled her eyes. 'Well if we're going to be together forever I can't exactly start now can I?'

'Oh for fuck's sake,' I said. 'You really are batshit crazy.'

Catherine lifted my chin so I was staring into her green feline eyes. What insane universe lay beyond them?

'Cheer up,' she said, stroking my cheek. 'You're the man I'm going to marry.'

And with that she ran out the door and into the Melbourne night.

The Hell Train

I once asked my father why he had had so many wives. I had expected a vague or glib explanation such as 'that's life' or 'well, it was the sixties …' But instead he paused for thought and looked at me with rare solemnity, as though assessing whether I was ready for his next words.

'The thing is,' he said finally, 'when it comes to love you have no choice. If there's chemistry there, there's nothing you can do. You've just got to get on board and ride the Hell Train.'

Greg Hildebrand might not have been a good man, but he was a wise man. When it came to Catherine it was true: I had no choice. Cautious diplomacy had failed; it was time for war. I vowed that night in my darkened house to use every skill, every argument and every dirty trick my young underdeveloped brain could conceive of to make Catherine mine. The Hell Train was leaving the station.

Early victories were few and Pyrrhic. For example, the following evening as we were walking down the street I managed, after fifteen or sixteen attempts, to engineer it so that our hands accidentally brushed each other's. I felt a spark jump between our fingers like Adam receiving the touch of God, and thus animated Catherine spun around to face me. However just as our heads inclined to meet one another she stopped to observe that I had something stuck between my teeth.

This incident was to set the tone for the whole campaign. Every time I had a chance cruel fate would intervene: Her friends would drop by to take her out, her mother would ring to tell her to come home or her suspiciously attractive English houseguest Preston would suddenly materialise in my lounge room. After weeks and then months of attack and defeat, offensive and counter-offensive, it was clear the War on Catherine could never be won. Much like the War on Terror of a decade later I was fighting an enemy who was rarely seen and who could always retreat into an environment which I could never infiltrate. I was, simply, not of her world.

Yet even as I felt I was slipping further away she was gradually drawing me closer. One night after uni she invited me back to her parents' house for dinner. It looked to me a mansion. We held hands under the table as I ate some strangely marinated Indian chicken and she sternly chastised me for not being a vegetarian. I played the giant old piano in the hall while she listened attentively and her father complained about the noise. And then we both went to bed, her in her peach-coloured room floating high above the house somewhere and me on a couch in the rumpus room upon which I slept not a wink.

In the morning I saw her in her white towelling dressing gown as she shuffled sleepily through the kitchen in search of the coffee machine. Her make-up was all gone and it left her pale face as small and featureless as a baby mouse. For the first time I could see what she really looked like. This was the face I had been searching for in all those long days and nights since she'd stepped into that crowded lift and here it was: a blank confused canvas.

That, I thought to myself, is my girlfriend. Whether she knows it or not.

And so the great romance sprung forth, as they all do, from small and unseen things. And just as surely it soon began to unravel in the face of large and unmissable ones.

Primarily I would sulk broodingly when Catherine didn't return my Herculean displays of devotion. However, in an effort to be reasonable I was always careful to counterbalance this with wild outbursts of jealousy over her many past lovers. Of course in retrospect this was foolish and immature – I should have been far more worried about her prospective ones.

The problem with paranoia is that it occasionally becomes true. Even in its embryonic stages our relationship was littered with various 'breaks' and break-ups, which meant that prospective lovers often quickly turned into current ones, who then turned into past ones, who would then end up in a framed photograph on her bedside table.

Or at least so I had cause to fear: Already there was a small pictorial army of exes mounted next to her nightlight, with James at its head. From this vantage point he and the ones before him would gaze out at me as I sought to engage Catherine's nocturnal attention. Needless to say, such attempts were not always successful.

Ultimately of course we were both just dumb kids flailing around in a big new world, me trying to shake off my past and her trying to hold onto hers. And that was the rub: I was embarrassed about the things I had done and the person I'd been but she was proud. To her the world was not quite as big nor as new. She had had more lovers than me, been to more parties than me, known more people than me and been to more countries than me – which is to say more than one. To me the city and the uni and the life that went with it might have been incredibly exciting but it was also terrifying and unknown. To her it had always been a playground.

I mean for God's sake, she'd even eaten in *restaurants*. Until I'd left home I hadn't even known I was allowed in one. And as far as keeping an ex-boyfriend hall of fame next to your bed was concerned, how was I to know that all eastern suburbs women didn't do the same? This was obviously how a mature and sophisticated person conducted their relationships and here I was just a backwards hick from the suburbs with unchecked emotions and a primitive notion of true love.

Everything I knew – Dandenong, my mother, Ash the Bogan – was so far away it might as well have existed in another dimension. Everything that had been normal to me was quaint and parochial and inferior to her and everything I pretended to be never quite fitted in. Just when I thought I had broken into a whole new realm I realised that I didn't belong there. I was an outsider at the bottom of society and an outsider at the top and that could mean only one thing.

Society must fall.

Children of the Revolution

It was not long after my discovery that Catherine was not just my girlfriend but my socio-economic oppressor that she dumped me, thus completing her victimisation of the proletariat. Yet such was her capo-fascist wiliness that she didn't so much break up with me as decree that we would both be better off being single. This subtle distinction meant that while we were no longer going out, we could still hang out together and even have sex on occasion. It also apparently meant that she could shag other men with impunity and drop by my house and introduce me to them.

But when she came by ahead of an evening out with one particular male friend I needed no introduction.

'Hi Joe,' she said breezily on the doorstep as I momentarily froze. 'You know Danny don't you?'

There standing next to her was a decidedly less comfortable Danny Bertossa.

'Er, yeah,' he confirmed on both our behalfs. 'G'day Joe.'

He reminded me of my father more than ever.

There was of course a reason for Danny's unease. Unlike Catherine, he knew exactly what was going to happen that night. Indeed, out of the three of us Catherine was the only one who didn't.

Ironically it was Danny, not Catherine, who was currently in a long-term committed relationship, but it was also Danny, not Catherine, who had the capacity to plan more than fifteen seconds ahead. There was no plot he couldn't anticipate ten steps in advance and he knew long before he saw my face that this was another powerplay he was destined to win.

And yet he was almost sorrowful about it, as though he was just a helpless pawn in a pre-ordained gameplan. Having observed the set-up and all the pieces in play he couldn't help but foresee its disastrous and inevitable conclusion, just as he himself would be powerless to escape his destiny. Like Greg Hildebrand he knew there would be no choice: The Hell Train came for all of us.

I too knew its inevitable course and so I retreated to my room in Palmerston Street that night with that sickly turning feeling, like falling in a dream.

In the wake of such misadventures, it was Catherine's custom to seek out my company that I might either reassure her with my blind devotion that she was not a bad person or angrily extract the confession she yearned to make. Foolishly, I regularly obliged on both counts.

The inevitable phone call the next day was received at my grandmother's house, where yet another family gathering was being despoiled by my romantic obsessions and the mysterious other life I now carried with me back home. I had not just contaminated the illustrious grounds of Melbourne University and the leafy eastern suburbs with my unclean presence, I had also brought the vain and hedonistic squabbles of bohemia back to the still and simple surrounds of our Dandenong cocoon. Wherever I went, it seemed, I was a virus.

My mother was grossly displeased that on one of the ever-decreasing few occasions I was supposed to see her and the family I had spent the whole time on the phone with Catherine in various states of consolation and distress. While she had always had a great deal of affection for the tall and ungainly beauty I had once or twice dared to bring home, she was convinced that our lines were unentwinable, the chasm between our two families impossible to cross.

Catherine on her inaugural trip to my mother's house had been both stunning and stunned. While she had not an ounce of pretension in her – her wayward psyche precluded her from sustaining affectation – she could not help but be confronted by the piles of clutter looming from all directions and at one point even attempted to do the dishes. This particular chore had defeated all members of our family for years and she retreated almost immediately. However, my mother, still unaware that her way of living was not entirely normal, took Catherine's valiant attempt at rectitude as a sign that such a clash of cultures could only end in tears.

Certainly that prediction was realised when she caught me on the phone that Sunday afternoon, and yet even then my distress was strangely mild. So conditioned was I to Catherine's myriad and ever-changing rules of engagement that even the day after she'd been fooling around with Danny Bertossa I struggled to identify where the precise breach of contract had occurred.

Soon I was asking and then begging and then demanding that my mother drive me the 40 kilometres to Ivanhoe, where an obliquely remorseful Catherine had requested my presence with a not quite legally binding suggestion that perhaps it might lead to us getting back together. My mother, by this stage as broken down and defeated as I was, ultimately complied.

One of my first duties as Catherine's newly reappointed boyfriend was to address the fact that Danny's girlfriend – an influential force in student politics herself – suddenly no longer wanted to be friends with her. This, Catherine felt, was highly unreasonable on her part, given that Danny was the one who'd done the cheating – especially when they'd only really had a bit of a snog. It was hardly fair that Kate freeze her out of social and political favour just because her boyfriend couldn't keep his cock in his pocket.

Catherine's solution to this was to have me speak to Danny and make him show Kate the error of her folly. Her reasoning was that I could explain to him that she'd screwed me over and I'd got over it, surely Kate should do the same.

Being night-time I was obviously some combination of drunk and stoned when I agreed to this course of action, however it would be disingenuous of me to make excuses. Frankly there are species of plants that have displayed more intelligence than I did around Catherine, and I should know because I probably smoked them.

And so I nodded my head and walked the few hundred metres from Palmerston Street to the student union rave party at which Kate had so inexplicably brushed her a few hours before. I saw Danny outside and barrelled up with righteous indignation. Why, I asked, was his girlfriend treating Catherine so callously when it was he who was to blame for the whole situation? Was this the social justice we had fought so passionately for?

Perhaps understandably, Danny was rather baffled by my line of questioning, not least because I was talking to him at all. Undeterred I pressed on.

'I mean she's back together with you and you're the one who cheated on her but she's not talking to Catherine. It just doesn't make any sense.'

Danny looked at me with the sort of curiosity that I imagined a dead animal might arouse in a veterinarian or perhaps a psychopathic killer.

'Can I just get this straight?' he asked rather clinically. 'Catherine cheated on you with me, then told you about it and then got you to come here and tell me to tell my girlfriend – whom I cheated on with Catherine – that she had to be nicer to her.'

'Well, technically we were on a break …' I mumbled.

'Wow,' Danny said. 'Look, I know it's probably not my place to give you advice right now but I've got to tell you man: That is seriously fucked up.'

I stood there in silence as my brain struggled to invert the world around me. Could it be that Catherine was not the baseline measure of relationship normality? Could it be that even among the children of the well-heeled and well-read upper middle class love and monogamy and jealousy were still the same emotions? Could it be that I was normal after all?

The fluorescent lights outside Union House flickered like lightning as Danny smoked a cigarette and waited for our conversation to end. But it had already ended.

I stalked home feeling both humiliated and vindicated as a cold Melbourne spring rain started spitting from the sky. When I walked through the door Catherine was there waiting, eager for news.

'How did it go?' she asked.

'Well,' I said, wiping water from my face, 'it was interesting.'

'What do you mean interesting?' she said. 'What happened? How did it turn out?'

I looked at her sitting perched and alert on the lip of the couch. I'd just been to Hell and back and she wanted to know how she'd gone in her job interview.

'It turned out,' I said, 'that you're even more fucking crazy than I thought.'

As I walked out of the room and trudged up the stairs to bed I finally accepted my last truth of the night. I would never change Catherine. Far easier to change the world.

The Apprentice

The Melbourne University student union was run much like the country itself, which is to say poorly but with the best of intentions. Indeed its power structure closely mirrored that of the hybrid Westminster–American style apparatus that rules us all.

The executive government was composed of office bearers who were elected individually on a two-party preferred basis, much like seats in the House of Representatives. The roles of president and general secretary were something akin to prime minister and treasurer, the often shared position of 'education vice-president' was immediately below that and was the favoured office of whatever powerbrokers were really in charge, and then there were a host of positions below ranging from arts officer (think abstract sculpture installations) to activities officer (think free beer after protests) to women's officer (think militant lesbians).

The executive was answerable to a legislative oversight body called the Student Council elected by a proportional quota system like the Senate. This was the supreme governing body to which either failed or former office bearers traditionally gravitated in order to cut deals, pass budgets and generally practise playing politics until they were hopefully drafted into the major leagues.

Council also oversaw the management of the student union, which is to say the vast body of staff who actually ran the building, its shops and its various services and kept the whole business staying afloat. Needless to say that is of no concern to us here.

Far more important were the T-shirts.

To be clear, we are not just talking about any old T-shirt here. This was a piece of fabric whose colour, cut, design and every possible socio-political implication therefrom was conceived, proposed and debated so exhaustively that it resulted in the longest caucus meeting Left Focus had ever had.

In the end we settled on a lilac affair adorned with the finest screen-printed cartoon daisy the people's money could buy. At the insistence of the more slender and well-proportioned activists in the group one version was a figure-hugging Bonds-style number, while in order to uphold our sworn declamation against sexism, homophobia and unrealistic body image ideals, we also produced looser sizes for the more pear-shaped computer nerds and fuller-bodied feminists. Even so, we had an election to win and it is with a heavy heart that I confess several union rules regarding the misogynist objectification of the female form were breached by that garment.

Thus adorned, Left Focus cast aside the Liberals with whom it had so uncomfortably shared power and won a clean sweep of every single executive office-bearer position. However, even once the T-shirt had done its job, all our bright-eyed and well-dressed radicals were still ultimately ruled by Student Council, and Council was no friend of the left. It was largely dominated by conservative third-year students who had either let off their revolutionary steam or never had any in the first place.

The numbers were held by a loose majority of Liberals, international students and an ever-present representative or two from the More Beer party, which everybody but the engineering students knew was a Liberal front. One councillor was Kelly O'Dwyer, now the Liberal member for Peter Costello's old seat of Higgins – a fact which I still find uncommonly arousing.

This was, as the student union's forefathers had intended, the perfect balance: The staff got their wages paid, the right could pretend they were still in charge and the left had something to protest against. Everybody was happy.

But then something terrible happened. Having been in power for a whole 12 months on their own without quite managing to screw everything up, Left Focus swept to victory again in the elections for the following year, holding on to every single office-bearing position. Yet in doing so committed the greatest mistake any political party can make: They won too much.

For the first time ever, the left had obtained a majority on Student Council, meaning not only that the union was run by the left but that the left running the union was also run by the left.

The one vital rule of politics is that the left must never achieve total power. For the left is a movement of protest, of railing against the dominant forces of evil it perceives everywhere. If the left becomes a dominant force itself it is immediately robbed of its entire purpose. It either ends up railing against the sky above it and flying too close to the sun or turning on itself to search for oppressors within – it cannot conceive of itself as ruling because to rule is in violation of its very essence.

This is why right-wing dictatorships flourish and left-wing dictatorships either founder or become right-wing ones. The right is comfortable with power, its members assume it to be their natural providence. But when the left attains power a kind of excited panic always sets in. It is much like a dog with a stick. First the dog is apoplectic that it cannot get the stick, then the dog chases after the stick with ferocious zeal, and then when the dog gets the stick it has no idea what to do with it. Eventually the dog either carries the stick back to its master in the hope that he will wave it around and throw it again or it just goes completely feral.

In the golden age of Ancient Rome, a republic run by high-minded idealistic aristocrats not unlike the inner-city intelligentsia of our day, the constitution actually made provision for dictatorships. When there was a major crisis to be dealt with and the usual squabbling self-interest of the Senate and its consuls invariably failed to address it, a single man would be appointed to fix the problem. It was, to be sure, a high-risk concept and yet from it flowed all the great names we know today, from Cincinnatus to Marius to Sulla to Caesar himself.

The great luck of Rome was that every time the republic was faced with a world-ending threat to its very existence it managed to find someone to save it. They always had a Caesar. We had Danny Bertossa.

Danny of course had been the one whose exceptional deal-making and electioneering skills had led to the left winning far more than it had ever expected or wanted. And yet it seemed that even despite himself he had engineered a way out of his own perfect problem.

Unbeknownst to most of his comrades, Danny had done a quiet deal with the International Students Association. The ISA were the left's sworn enemies, a bit of casual racism excused by the fact they were the offspring of overseas doctors and lawyers – the chief crime in that being they stole university places from the offspring of local doctors and lawyers. In a deft move, Danny had convinced the ISA to give Left Focus their preferences for all the executive positions in exchange for the last spot on Left Focus's Student Council ticket, which he secretly knew to be unwinnable.

It was therefore a somewhat awkward moment when Left Focus not only won all the office-bearing positions in its own right but did indeed pick up the final spot on Council, and with it control of Council itself. The more junior members of caucus – unaware that according to the first law of politics this would signal their own doom – were overjoyed. But the rapture subsided into confusion when it emerged that the successful final candidate was a young man by the name of Wang Hu whom nobody could seem to remember coming to any meetings.

Amid puzzled looks around the caucus room – a largish carpeted premises in Union House in which everybody sat on the floor in a circle – Danny and his senior lieutenants exchanged worried glances and then suddenly left to attend to urgent union business. Soon the circle was beset by – if you can forgive the expression – Chinese whispers that Danny had not only offered the ISA Left Focus's last spot on the Council ticket, but actually got an international student to pose as a Left Focus member for the duration of the campaign.

'You mean,' said one outraged feminist a little too loudly, 'he was wearing one of our *T-shirts*?'

For the first time ever caucus turned on Danny Bertossa, its leader, its mentor and its father. A counter-revolution seemed imminent.

But it was not for nothing that Danny had established a new party and then led it to its greatest victory, even if it was one so great that it threatened to overwhelm him. Politics is nothing if not the art of persuasion and he was the undisputed master of that.

Away from the collective consternation of caucus he managed to persuade the jittery leadership group – of which he was, naturally, the leader – that this was the price of victory. Besides, he reminded them, they had all agreed to it. If he was going down it would not be alone. Sure, he might have done a deal on the side but that was only to ensure that Left Focus maintained its monopoly on the office-bearing positions – and hadn't they done that? The fact that they had done it without the need for the ISA preferences he had sold them down the river for only proved once more, he beseeched them, that he was a victim of his own success.

With Danny's golden tonsils and silver tongue the battle was not long fought. The leadership group assuaged, they placated the rest of the caucus and party unity was restored – although Danny and his two co-conspirators would forever be known as 'the Junta'.

Within all these unseemly machinations it had almost been forgotten that Left Focus had achieved yet another record result when the second-last name on the ticket got through. For the first time in the university's history a first-year student had been elected to Student Council. He was a thoughtful, pragmatic and quick-minded young man by the name of Matthew Lennox.

Danny Bertossa had found his apprentice.

Absolute Power

With all the pieces in place and all the chips in hand Left Focus had set the stage for a progressive protest-staging regime that would reign for a thousand years.

But how does one turn 100 per cent into 110 per cent? How does one turn everything into more? In answer to this Danny Bertossa came up with an idea that would have made Machiavelli put down his pen and stare at the wall. Napoleons asked how to win absolute power. Caesars asked how to win absolute power forever.

Wiser political strategists obsess over this: not just how to gain power, but how to perpetuate it. It is said that the greatest acts of the five good emperors of Rome – Nerva, Trajan, Hadrian, Antoninus Pius and Marcus Aurelius – were not their conquests, oratories or wise administration but choosing the right heir. The best rulers make provisions not for today but for tomorrow.

And so Danny Bertossa took under his wing the young Matthew Lennox and taught him all that he had learned, and warned him of the mistakes he had made. The books, the tricks, the people and the tactics were all passed down to him like father to son. When Danny left, as he inevitably would for a high-powered Labor Party gig or union job, his entire body of knowledge would rest within his protégé and with it the fate of Left Focus.

That achieved, it was time to give his young prince a castle, a political fortress that would be impenetrable.

Most political operatives are consumed by what their party needs to say, what it needs to do; its internal workings, its external messages; its people, its policies, its leaders, its supporters. All these things are necessary to win office.

But what if you changed the nature of the office itself, so that only your party could win it? What if there were democratically elected positions that only your party could fill? What if you made it impossible for your opposition to even field a candidate?

And so it was announced in February that Left Focus had, in the interests of positive and progressive representation, created three new positions: Welfare Officer, Environment Officer and Queer Officer.

The Libs were flummoxed: They didn't believe in welfare, they didn't believe in the environment and they couldn't even find a Liberal who was queer – or at least who would admit to it. Their only option was to run candidates who vowed, if elected, to abolish their own positions. Even in the postmodern world of student politics this was a difficult message to sell.

The only question was who among us would be campaign manager for the massive triple by-election required to fill these newly invented offices. At first blush such an unloseable proposition would seem a gift to any party operative but after the exhausting rigours of the campaign a few short months ago and its troublesome aftermath the experienced hands were weary of electioneering and wanted to get on with the job of basking in their spoils.

Besides, what self-respecting political guru could be bothered delivering a foregone conclusion? There was no point wasting a genuine talent on a job that could be done by an organ grinder's monkey. All they needed was the monkey itself.

Naturally, with Danny and Matt doing the numbers, the vote for campaign manager was a foregone conclusion – I didn't even know I was running until I'd been elected unanimously. Chuffed at the honour, I was about to give a humble acceptance speech when a second vote was immediately called stipulating that I could only take the role on the strict proviso that I would be closely supervised throughout by Matt Lennox. It says something about my comrades' regard for me that even when put in charge of a plan whose very essence was that it was unfuckupable they still had their doubts.

I looked around the caucus room to find my new boss, who was sitting impassively in a long black trenchcoat. He shrugged his shoulders and muttered 'yep', then shepherded me out of the room like a mafia hitman ushering an unsuspecting mark to a creek bed.

Being the diligent professional that he was, Matt Lennox had already consulted widely about the type of person I was: my strengths and weaknesses, pedigree and ambitions, personal failings and potential risks. This background check completed, he finally asked Danny Bertossa.

'He's fine,' Danny said breezily. 'I think he'll go well.'

'But I heard you guys weren't talking,' Matt said, knowing Danny would be proud he had done his homework.

'Good catch,' he said. 'But don't worry, it's not political. It's just 'cause I had a little thing with Catherine when they were going out. He's still funny about her.'

Matt paused. 'Hang on – did you say his ex was called Catherine?'

'Oh fuck,' Danny said. 'Don't tell me you …'

The Three-Week Plan

When you take away the deals and the double deals and the counter deals, winning a student election comes down to three things:

Week 1: Posters
Week 2: Posters and chalk
Week 3: Posters, chalk and lecture-bashing

This strategy was, if only marginally, more sophisticated than it might appear. Student elections were ultimately a teenage popularity contest on a larger scale. Whichever party seemed the most popular would inevitably become the most popular, which meant that to win you had to look like you were already winning. If you made it look like everyone was voting for your side then everyone would vote for your side. Peer pressure was and remains the most powerful manipulator of the human soul. People say that everybody goes for the underdog? Bullshit. People might like an underdog but they love a winner.

This meant getting out earlier and getting out bigger. When it came to posters, chalk and lecture-bashing you couldn't just do it, you had to do it faster, harder, cheaper and dirtier than anybody else.

And so to the posters. Because the left had all the office-bearing positions it meant we had all the offices, which in turn meant we had all the photocopiers. All we had to do was let ourselves in on a Sunday afternoon armed with a slab of lilac A3 paper and run off a thousand or so copies at a time. I thought this a rather mundane exercise for such top-flight campaign strategists as Matthew Lennox and myself until I noticed that Matt had locked the door behind us and slid a filing cabinet in front of it.

'Er, what are you doing?' I asked.

'What does it look like?'

'Are we not allowed in here?'

'Of course we're allowed in here,' he said, peering through the office windows into the corridor outside. 'We're just not allowed to do this in here.'

'But we run off posters all the time. Look at the bloody walls.'

'They're student union posters. These are Left Focus posters.'

'But we are the student union.'

'Not at election time we're not.'

'How come?'

'Because,' Matt sighed, 'elections are supposed to be fair.'

Once we had the posters there was of course the matter of posting them but again it wasn't that simple. The only places where posters were allowed were the large concrete bollards scattered around campus, and each of these was governed by more bureaucracy than the complaints department at the ABC.

Firstly, it was strictly forbidden to tear down other parties' posters – parties were not even supposed to cover other posters with their own. The trick therefore was to plaster every bollard with propaganda before anybody else got to it – hence 'Week 1: Posters'.

Once that was done the key was to have scouts constantly patrolling the campus in order to catch your opponents covering, cleansing or otherwise defacing the smothered bollards, as they would inevitably be forced to do. Then you simply reported them to the returning officer, getting the offending party branded as cheaters and its operatives suspended from the campaign.

This strategy was not foolproof. While parties were not supposed to cover their opponents' posters with their own, there was a clause that this was only if there was 'available space' on the bollard. For this purpose we would always leave the bottom 20 inches or so uncovered by Left Focus livery so the opposition would have to stick their posters on an almost subterranean level but be unable to complain we hadn't left them any room to exercise their democratic right. Fights thus quickly erupted over the definition of 'available space' and the poster wars began.

By the end of Week 1 it would become an all-out frenzy of plastering, tearing down and plastering again until one of the many paradoxes of student politics arose: You had to have your posters on first which meant that you had to have them on last. Because the clandestine act of ripping off posters could only be done under cover of darkness, the aim was to be the last party to do a poster run each night so that yours would be the message emblazoned across campus when everybody arrived in the morning.

In this the left had a clearly unfair advantage. As our campaign team was composed almost entirely of arts students there were very few academic or workplace commitments to prevent us doing poster runs at three o'clock in the morning, a time when the Libs had to be sound asleep in preparation for the next day's commerce lectures. Or indeed on weekends, when the protestant work ethic of our rival undergraduates meant they had to attend to their part-time jobs.

Still, the rules were so openly flouted that by the end of a campaign there was often a small orderly queue of activists waiting patiently for the opponent in front of them to finish doing his postering so that they could cover it up immediately upon his departure – a fate to which the unlucky posterer was resigned as he did his pointless duty. By that stage it was not uncommon for bollards to be eight or ten posters deep at the end of the day. It was, appropriately enough for Melbourne fashion sensibilities, an orgy of layering.

Chalking, on the other hand, did not seem to provoke the same level of emotion and occasional violence that posters did, at least not since the great Chalk Paint Controversy of 1993. This was when some forward-thinking political leaders had coated the university's footpaths with a new colour compound that was almost impossible to remove and which was still there by the time I arrived a year later, advocating a vote for some long bygone party whose logo might as well have been a cave drawing.

Legend had it that when confronted by angry opponents and groundskeepers, these ancient activists had declared the substance was 'chalk paint', and therefore completely legal under union rules. The authorities begged to differ and came to the view that the 'chalk paint' was in fact 'paint', thus consigning that particular artistic technique to history.

As a result of this landmark ruling the more conventional 'chalk chalk' we were allowed to use lasted only a week at most. However, we discovered that by applying a thick enough coat and then wetting it we could make it seep into and cling to the concrete and thus double its life expectancy. This meant that a well-laid motif would still be visible when the polls opened in the third and final week. Hence, not to put too fine a point on it, 'Week 2: Posters and chalk'.

And then, God help us all, there was lecture-bashing.

Walking the Talk

'Okay,' said Matt Lennox. 'Go for it.'

The next thing I knew I was standing in front of 500 people in one of the uni's biggest lecture halls. It hadn't seemed so big when I was dozing off in the back row. Suddenly I now saw how far away that back row was and how close was the row right in front of me. The audience was huge and I was small and then everything went blank.

I later learned I had stammered out a few words about how Left Focus was, 'like, really good' and voluntary student unionism was 'like, really bad' but none of this was revealed until after I had staggered off the stage and into the alcove behind it, where Matthew was struggling to disguise his distress.

It was D-day, the last week of the campaign. The polls were open and the vote was on. The posters and chalk had done their duty but they couldn't finish the job. A piece of paper or an image on the ground could plant the seed but it couldn't walk a voter across the line. A person needed fire in the belly to propel their legs to a cardboard booth and put a number in a box. They needed a reason. The poster told them what to vote for and the chalk told them who.

Now the lecture-bash was supposed to tell them why and I was a man without a voice. Without Week 3 everything was lost.

Sparing the usual reassurances, Matt yanked my quivering arm and dragged me away from the scene of the crime, planting my unsteady rear in a chair at the nearest coffee shop he could find.

After I'd gathered enough time and distance I pressed a watery cappuccino to my lips and dared to suggest: 'Well, I guess that wasn't so bad …'

Matt shot me a reproachful stare and I looked down at the cup apologetically.

'It was fucking awful and you know it,' he said.

I nodded.

'But it's not your fault.'

'Then whose fault is it? The system's?'

'Hah. No, it's not even the system's fault. It's pretty much the only thing that's not the system's fault. It's my fault. With all your bullshit I just assumed you knew what you were doing.'

'*I* assumed I knew what I was doing.'

'Yeah, but it's your job to assume that. It's my job to assume you don't. It's my fuck-up.'

'So what do I do?'

'Well,' he said, 'I'm glad you finally fucking asked.'

With that Matt Lennox swept the coffee cups to one side with a meaty forearm, the better to bang the table with.

'Firstly, you never just rock up and start talking shit. You say hello – it's only manners. And what happens when you say hello to someone?'

'They say hello back?'

'Right. That means you're not just talking to them anymore, you're having a conversation. And in conversations people listen. It's not a speech anymore, it's a dialogue – just a dialogue in which you do all the talking.'

'And then what?'

'Exactly. Ask them a question. But a question that you know the answer to, a question to which your whole speech is the answer – Are you sick of upfront fees? Do you like free beer? Did anyone spew their guts up at the Law Ball? Simple shit. That reminds me – hit your targets. If it's an arts class make a joke about bongs, if it's an engineering class make a joke about beer, if it's an economics class make a joke about – I dunno – John Maynard Keynes.'

'But what about the politics. What about what we're doing?'

'No – never tell them what *we're* doing – only tell them what we're doing *for them*. Remember, it's voluntary voting. They're only going to get out and drop in the box if they're wide-eyed revolutionaries or they think there's something in it for them. And if they're wide-eyed revolutionaries they're already ours, so always always always make it about them.'

'Right,' I said. 'It's all about them.'

'But it's also all about us. They have to like you. Remember when you were the nerd in high school?'

'Er, no.'

Matt laughed. 'Yeah, whatever. And there was the cool group that you always wanted to get into but never could?'

I sighed. 'Yeah.'

'Well right now, we *are* the cool group. The only difference is anybody can join. We're taking every nerd, every geek, everyone who ever felt left out and giving them a chance to be popular for the first time in their lives. We're shaving off the pack to make a bigger pack. We're letting the meek finally inherit the Earth. You've got to be cool, be desirable, make them want to come to us.'

'Okay ...' I said.

'Good. But if they don't want to come to us the most important thing is that they don't come at all. Two-thirds of students are Tories. The only reason we're in power is because they don't give a shit and they don't vote and we have to keep it that way. We aren't running against the Libs, we're running against nothing. Vote for us or don't vote at all. They're the two choices we have to put out. You get it?'

'Got it,' I said.

'Oh, and there's one more thing you need to know.'

'What's that?'

'I'm sorry I fucked Catherine.'

* * *

The next day Matt Lennox put me in front of an even bigger lecture theatre, this one full of medical students. When you're studying the power of life and death – or indeed studying at all – the question of who is going to be the inaugural Melbourne University Queer Officer tends not to capture your attention. The vast majority of med students treated student politics with either indifference or contempt and the ones who didn't voted Liberal.

As was customary, I walked up to the lecturer, who was still arranging his slides, and asked if I might have a quick word with his students. Lecturers were supposed to say 'Of course' with a nostalgic smile and wave the young ideologue to the lectern. However, this one was a thin-lipped old professor with the moral bearing of a Dickensian debt collector who snapped that he did in fact mind so I'd better hurry up.

I approached the stand and with my winningest smile said: 'Hi, I'm Joe Hildebrand from Left Focus. How you guys doing today?'

In response a pen, a few scrunched-up balls of paper, a piece of chalk and several other unidentified missiles were hurled at me from great height. I was noting with some bitterness that Matt Lennox's exhaustive training had not covered this particular scenario when a late and low-flying projectile hit me in the thigh.

'Geez, that hurt,' I said, scratching my leg in what I hoped was a rather nonchalant manner. 'I don't suppose there's a doctor in the house?'

A small titter trickled from the back of the dark cavernous room.

'Don't worry, it's fine,' I said. 'I just came from Engineering. They threw beer cans.'

This time there was a solid chuckle.

'Yeah it was tough. I just wish they had've emptied them first.'

Now, finally, the bastards laughed.

'Look,' I said, 'it's true I do try to get shit thrown at me at least once a day but the other reason I'm here is to tell you about voluntary student unionism. Have you guys heard of that?'

I could see a few nods. Not many, but enough.

'Alright. Well, the thing is it sounds all nice and friendly and "free association" and all that crap and it might even look good on paper. Or you might not care what it looks like because you don't think it matters to you – and that's fair enough. They don't want you to think it matters to you. The problem is that it does, so I'm here just to let you know why and then you can decide what to do about it.'

I paused while I struggled to think of any possible reason a rich med student could possibly benefit from the union. Matt's stirring speech from the mount had certainly been light on specifics.

'Okay,' I said at last. 'So the student union has a deal going with the medical centre just across the road. Say you luck out at the specialist's position at St Vincent's and end up there – *cha-ching!* Every time a kid rocks up that's money in your pocket.'

The response was less than overwhelming. Clearly few med students dreamed of a life handing out morning-after pills to wayward college girls.

'You know what else we do for the medical profession?' I said. 'We hold protests every single week – sometimes every day. We're talking about a constant stream of injured socialists who've been stomped on by police horses. Imagine all the bulk-billing for that.'

This got a little laugh but I had nothing left. It was clear to me the student union really didn't do shit for these guys. I needed something more, something that struck at their very sense of self. But what the Hell did I know about the medical profession?

Only one thing.

'And you know what else? The student union operates a dental surgery. Every time – oh sorry, I forgot I was talking to real doctors.'

And with that the place erupted.

'Yeah, that's right,' I said. 'And we're also campaigning against upfront fees, so that even your massively rich parents don't have to pay for you to go to university. So you can go out and get pissed on the weekend instead of having to push plates at a shitty little café just because your dad says it's character building. And we're doing all this for you. Because even though you hate us, we love you. And if you don't care about any of this, no problem – don't vote. And if you do care all you have to do is vote for us.'

I paused again to catch my breath and tried to steady my quivering hands by gripping the sides of the lectern.

'Either way,' I said, 'it won't make any difference. We'll be fighting for your rights whether you like it or not.'

There was a second's silence. Then the room exploded with applause.

When the votes were counted at the end of the week Left Focus had won all three positions by up to 90 per cent of the student ballot. Now it was time to take on the rest of the world.

The Revolution Cometh

If the election result was the full stop of Left Focus's quest for victory then the by-election was three exclamation marks at the end, like a text message written by an overexcited tween. There was no way in which we could have more emphatically asserted our dominance over the student union. That done, we turned our minds to casual displays of supremacy, as sure a sign of the corrupting temptations of power as ever there was.

On what could at best be described as a whim, Left Focus decided to roll an admittedly annoying and foppish Young Laborite called Andrew Giles, whose crime against the revolution had been to found a more moderate party called Broad Left. The concept of any kind of moderation, in life or in politics, was of course completely foreign to us and what couldn't be understood naturally had to be destroyed.

Giles was running for the presidency of the ALP Club, a group of which he had been an active member for several years and whose operation and existence bore no threat to Left Focus or its ongoing control of the union. Still, he had to be stopped, even if for no other reason than that we could stop him.

The process was simple enough: Left Focus officers went around with a clipboard seeking the two-dollar membership fee to sign everyone up to the Labor Club. If they didn't have the two dollars that was obviously no problem – the officers, or perhaps ultimately their parents, just paid it themselves. I, however, was more than happy to pay my way. I had always wanted to join the Labor Party, and what more honourable and fitting way to do it than for the purposes of a branch stack.

As it was about twenty of us marched in to the ALP Club meeting room just as Andrew Giles was concluding his candidate's speech. Upon seeing his fate writ large in the procession of lilac T-shirts he put his notes aside and instead embarked upon a genuinely moving oration using words such as 'disgrace' and 'gross abuse of process' and various other familiar terms.

Minutes later the vote was taken, he lost, and we walked straight back out again. Having dealt with the counter-revolutionary elements on campus, it was now time to take our movement to the streets.

The rally was, as all rallies were, against voluntary student unionism. This one, however, was going to be big. The Howard government had just been elected in a landslide, thus wiping out Paul Keating's student union bailout package, and there was little doubt that the apocalypse was nigh.

Of course we had had many protest marches before – too many to name or remember – but none of them had made the slightest amount of difference. The lesson from this was clear to all of us: We had to have more protest marches.

The rally was to begin at the State Library, where all rallies began, and make its way to State Parliament, where all rallies ended, although this habit was immaterial to which particular tier of government we were protesting against. Not only did the steps of the Victorian Parliament House make a convenient amphitheatre but the odds were that no matter which government building we marched on we could always find someone who was oppressing us. That being a given, we figured we might as well go with the one we knew.

On this day the plan was that once assembled on the steps everyone would be given a cardboard mask depicting the face of Jeff Kennett, our almost familial arch-nemesis and the architect of the voluntary student unionism scheme we felt sure would destroy us. We would then ask everyone to don their masks and stage a minute's silence to symbolically mark the death of student unions.

The idea was the brainchild of new vice-president Felicity Martin, a blue-eyed brunette born-again socialist who looked uncommonly attractive in the figure-hugging Left Focus T-shirt – not that that, the male comrades agreed, had anything to do with anything.

Leading the protest was a job that even a monkey could do and once more that monkey was me. I dutifully marshalled the troops outside the union building and then led them down Swanston Street to the stately lawns in front of the State Library, megaphone in hand. There we met with our fellow travellers from the other universities and commenced the en masse march to Parliament House. We were by this stage some 10,000 strong and felt that surely no democratic government could withstand our mighty display of people power or the inarguable logic of the words 'Hey hey! Ho ho! VSU has got to go!'

Not long afterwards I was atop the steps of Parliament House with 10,000 angry young souls teeming below. Among them the marshals were distributing the cardboard Kennett masks, whose crudely slashed slits for the eyes and mouth only rendered them all the more sinister. The protesters, being the untamable rebels they were, all put them on.

This accomplished, Felicity bade me take the microphone thus to produce the grand reveal and stun the world into enlightenment. I seized it with zeal.

'What we have come here to fight against,' I shouted through my own thin cardboard slot, 'is the most outrageous and unprecedented attack on students in the history of this state.'

A sonic swell of booing and hissing echoed back.

'The most terrible injustice ever visited upon young people today.'

More booing and hissing replied, this time accompanied by the unmistakable sound of an enthusiastically beaten bongo drum.

'We are witnessing the complete destruction of our way of being, the annihilation of our culture.'

The boos and hisses now twisted like a waterspout into a single howling moan and the bongo player damn near shit his pants.

'And so to mark this genocide, to mourn Jeff Kennett's murder of student life, I want you to all stand silent.'

I stood there and waited for the voices to still and sure enough there was at first a general hush. But soon a ripple of uncertain murmuring radiated through the crowd, accompanied by a confused turning of heads. Then came a lone squeaky voice from somewhere far off at the back of the crowd.

'No.'

This was, it must be said, not the response I had anticipated.

I mustered my sternest protest voice and tried again. 'I said, I want you all to be silent!'

The crowd bubbled and mumbled with more uncertainty and then seemed to turn as one back towards the lone voice, seeking further direction.

'Fuck off!' it squeaked again.

Much relieved to hear a more accessible instruction, a chorus of other voices now joined in: 'Get fucked! No way! Never! Fuck *you*!'

I glanced sideways at Felicity, who frantically attempted to mouth back what I presumed was the emergency escape plan, but unfortunately this was somewhat difficult to decipher because she, like everyone else, had a cardboard cut-out of Jeff Kennett's head on her face. As, indeed, did I.

It was then that I fully appreciated the conceptual conflict at the heart of our little piece of political street theatre. As far as the confused and angry protesters below were concerned I *was* Jeff Kennett. Granted this was only insofar as I was wearing a photocopied picture of him stuck on my face but these were student socialists I was dealing with. How were they to know the difference?

At least now I knew what I had to do. I turned back to the protesters and adopted as dictatorial a posture as possible for someone wearing cheesecloth pants.

'I said,' I shouted, 'I want you to be *SILENT!*'

'*NO!*' they shouted back in unison.

'You mean you won't be *SILENT?!?*'

'*NO!!!*' they shouted louder.

'Are we ever gonna be *SILENT again?!?*'

'*NOOOOO!!!!!*'

The mob was in a frenzy. I stepped back from the podium with roaring chants ringing in my ears while Felicity raced up, her crystal blue eyes sparkling in a way that a less enlightened feminist than myself might have found arousing.

'That was great,' she said. 'They're all revved up. Let's go.'

'Er, go where?' I said.

Felicity looked at me quizzically.

'What are you talking about?' she said. 'It's time for Plan B.'

* * *

If I had bothered to go to more of the organisers' meetings, or indeed known where they were being held, I would have learned that the true purpose for that day's rally had been not just a piece of performance art but also a mass occupation of Liberal Party headquarters. As it was I discovered this while being chased down the street by 10,000 radicals, which is a difficult time to digest new information.

Occupying things was and remains a key plank of any left-wing campaign strategy. The idea of an occupation is to invade a building belonging to an oppressive capitalist organisation (which is to say any building more than two storeys tall) and then sit there chanting with arms interlocked until forcibly removed by the police.

This achieves the twin objectives of A) Getting on the news; and B) Getting arrested. Of course in terms of actually changing whatever it is that's being protested against it doesn't achieve a thing, but if we'd allowed that consideration to distract us we would've never got anything done.

Occupying buildings was not a sophisticated form of political expression but it still required a basic level of preparation, not least of which was choosing a building to occupy. And so when I responded to the news that we were about to invade Liberal headquarters by asking, 'Where is that again?' it must be said my comrades' faces were not overly burdened by confidence.

'It's in Exhibition Street,' Felicity sighed.

And so with our troops restless and primed for battle I sprinted down into the fray, my hand tightly clasped around my megaphone, urging them to follow me to a place I knew not where. As I galloped down Exhibition Street such small concerns as these evaporated. I felt like I could run forever, and indeed was obliged to run forever if I wasn't going to be trampled by my comrades. So this, I supposed, was what the New World Order felt like. But then I hit a crossroads.

Unfortunately this was not a moral, political or existential crossroads but a literal one, specifically the intersection of Exhibition and Flinders streets. And while the cops had duly cleared Exhibition Street for the protest – even they were more aware of our protest route than I was – they had not accounted for a rogue megaphone-wielding revolutionary leading a charge of 10,000 youths into oncoming traffic at the next street down.

As it belatedly occurred to me that I was, at a conservative estimate, about to lead at least several hundred people to their deaths, I spun my head around looking for some point of reference and it was then I saw over my left shoulder some two dozen police mounted on horseback in front of the building we were currently running past. The cops had been bracing themselves for impact only to see the horde of rampaging ferals charge straight past them. I still remember them dropping their jaws and turning their heads in unison, like the oscillating clowns at a church fete, while the faint sound of Felicity's screams echoed in the background.

Psycho Journo

In the months that followed that fateful day Felicity Martin became a lesbian, and I was never asked to lead a protest again, although I see no reason why the two events were related.

But, like Felicity, I too experienced a conversion of sorts. When I dreamt of revolution it was of a world in which my mother no longer had to worry about money and Dandenong was no longer a shithole and people like me didn't feel embarrassed at restaurants. The process of achieving that utopia, however, was something to which I really hadn't given much thought. Certainly it appeared that storming buildings wasn't my forte.

As always in such soul-turning moments I turned to a higher power, someone who had been sent to Earth by their father to sacrifice themselves for the greater good of humanity. What, I wondered, would Superman do?

The answer of course was clear: He became a reporter.

And so I joined forces with three other students – Phip, Derek and Vanessa – in a bid to edit the student newspaper. Like anything else in the student union, editing the paper could be done only as a collective and only after that collective had been endorsed by caucus and then voted in by the student body.

My would-be co-editors were more passionate about font sizes than freeing East Timor, and so were nervous about the political process, labouring under the misguided illusion that it was in some way democratic. Even after being unanimously preselected by caucus, which was happy to do anything that might stop me from leading another protest march, Phip, Vanessa and Derek still fretted over the elections. Indeed, they were the only people involved in the whole process – including all those running against us – who thought there was the remotest chance we might not win.

As I listened to their charmingly naïve concerns around a table at the student union coffee shop it became clear that they were so anxious about losing that they might yet prove themselves correct. I had visions of Phip running up to voters with a harried expression on her face saying: 'Don't vote for us. We're not ready.'

And so, having spent days dismissing their questions with a wave of the hand and a don't-worry-it'll-be-fine, I tried a sudden reverse of tack.

'My God!' I said. 'You're right. We're all screwed.'

Oddly enough, this seemed to calm them all immediately.

'If only we had an emergency plan, some kind of secret weapon ...'

The other three all nodded, as if this was a profound solution in itself.

'I've got an idea,' I said. 'Wait here.'

Thirty seconds later I returned with Matt Lennox, who had been waiting on the other side of the door. Without so much as an introduction he eyeballed each of them one at a time and then said to the group: 'So, I hear you guys want to win an election?'

Once more the three of them nodded, impressed – how did he *know*?

'I see,' he said. 'Well look. I'm not supposed to tell you this but because Joe's a friend I'll let you in on a secret new campaign strategy we've been working on.'

He pulled out a blank sheet of paper and a pen and put them both on the table with solemn gravity. 'Phip, you might want to write this down.'

Phip obediently grabbed both and sat attentively with the pen poised.

'Okay,' Matt said. 'Week 1: *Posters* ...'

* * *

The name of the student newspaper was *Farrago* and we branded our ticket *Psycho Farrago*. The name was chosen because in 1990s Melbourne 'psycho' was the highest form of praise you could bestow upon someone – as in: 'Man, I can't believe you smoke bucket bongs in the shower. You're such a *psycho*' – and it rhymed, which was the quality any student politician admired most in a slogan.

The most important part of the campaign for media officers – the appropriately non-hierarchical title the student union gave the paper's editors – was to produce a test edition that would be handed out to voters. However the test edition was technically election material and so the problem remained that we were not allowed to produce it using student union resources. Nor was there any room for the sort of skullduggery we normally engaged in. Running off a few posters was one thing, running off a 16-page newspaper was quite another.

But, as Matt Lennox had thoughtfully pointed out, the rules only said we couldn't use our student union. They didn't say we couldn't use someone else's.

As it happened the left had also won control of RMIT that year and we were well acquainted with them through our collective work on various National Days of Action – which civilians might know better as 'Wednesdays'. And so Phip, Vanessa, Derek and I spent a furtive weekend locked in a poster-clad basement in the RMIT student union producing our first masterpiece.

My artistic vision was that the whole edition would be the exact size and shape of a 45rpm single, an idea so fresh and original that I was sure no one had ever even attempted such a design before. As it turned out this was true, largely because no one in Australia had a printing press that could process round pieces of paper. And also no one had any round pieces of paper.

Being nothing if not a man of vision, even when this slight hiccup in the production process was pointed out I would not be bowed. I simply declared that we would print it on square pieces of paper and then carefully cut them round with scissors. After all, it was only 2000 copies.

Tragically, not for the first time, the people were not with me that day and the subsequent vote was decided three to one that we would just print the newspaper on an A4 shape like everybody else did, although we did put a picture of a round 45rpm single on the front and we did cut off the bottom of each copy so as to make it square.

Thus I acquired my first taste of bitter compromise and my colleagues acquired their first taste of bitter resentment. It was as authentic a newspaper environment as one could hope for.

Even at that early stage my political and editorial acumen was already beginning to show. The main feature of the test edition was an eerily foresightful piece on a young newly elected MP by the name of Lindsay Tanner, who went on to become one of the leading minds of the Labor government. Unfortunately this article was entirely conceived of and executed by Phip, while I was trying to persuade the team that the real man to watch was an up-and-coming powerhouse called Phil Cleary, a left-wing independent whose name since then has most commonly been accompanied by the words: 'Whatever happened to that guy?'

I did however contribute two pieces to our test edition. One was an interview with Dorothy Porter, who being both a poet and a lesbian stood to attract up to 90 per cent of the arts student vote. The other was the debut of a bogus advice column by a character called Agony Aunt Agatha which was as widely read as it was relevant.

There inside an airless dungeon somewhere underneath Swanston Street we battled crashing servers, creeping deadlines and each other – primarily in arguments about fonts. Never has Arial Narrow come so close to provoking bloodshed.

Our sole source of nutrition was whatever we could negotiate from the vending machine with our limited funds and however many bongs I could sneak in the darkroom. Food was the least of our worries though. If we didn't get out of there before daybreak on Monday the whole operation would be blown – what we were doing might not have been against our union rules but it was sure as hell against RMIT's. Besides, if we didn't get the edition to print by 9am there was no way we could make the campaign launch. Never had a deadline been so vital, so final or so unyielding. And so we worked all day and night, with Monday morning pacing towards us like John Wayne.

* * *

Somehow we made deadline. Somehow people always do. And so with our test edition printed, our editing skills at the height of their powers and our campaign strategy unassailable, there was nothing to stop us taking over the world. The only thing left to do was to have a destructive all-consuming affair with one of my teammates.

This was, it must be remembered, university. To know someone for more than three days without snogging, shagging or at least secretly lusting after them was considered a great insult. And in the incestuous world of student politics such an insult was multiplied by a factor of ten. It was inevitable that someone would have to tear apart the team by having sex with the wrong person and in testimony to my selfless nature I graciously allowed that person to be me.

Phip was the most driven, neurotic and scary one of the four of us and so naturally I had contemplated sleeping with her. But she then went out with one of my best friends at the time, a wise and wiry former *Farrago* editor called Matthew Gingold who had played a vital role in getting our test edition off the ground. Even in a world where morality and social etiquette were more elastic than Clive Palmer's tracksuit pants it somehow just didn't feel right.

Likewise Derek was not an option. While he had long flowing hair, a big smile and great taste in music, he was inescapably male. As progressive and enlightened as I was, I still couldn't quite bring myself to topple that particular wall of social oppression.

That left Vanessa, an intellectual, open-minded, talented, creative and forward-thinking feminist who was, by happy coincidence, also rather hot.

Cardigan Street

At this time I was living in a share house in Cardigan Street, the previous place in Palmerston Street having, perhaps unsurprisingly, imploded under the weight of chronic drug use and sexual infidelity. The only survivors were Liv and myself, who staggered like refugees from house interview to house interview until we found ourselves sitting before a large engineering student called Darrin – and yes his parents really spelt it that way – waiting for him to pass judgment upon us.

'Well,' he said at length, 'the way I see it we've got two rooms going and there are two of you.'

This was a promising start.

'That's true,' I said. 'So …'

'So what?' Darrin asked.

'Er, so can we move in?'

'I don't care,' Darrin shrugged, as though surprised to be asked. 'You can do whatever you want.'

And that was that. Almost impossibly, Cardigan Street was even closer to campus than Palmerston Street and had if anything an even more concentrated stream of kids filing through day and night to fish around in the fridge for a loose beer or cautiously survey the remnants of the mix bowl for what might or might not – depending on one's outlook on life – constitute half a cone.

But while dope was always the primary drug of choice for myself and my fellow political and artistic expeditionaries, Darrin was a man of simpler tastes. Darrin, you see, liked beer.

Even this statement does not quite do credit to the relationship Darrin had with beer, which was unusually strong even for an engineering student. Not only did Darrin like beer, it seemed to like him back. It was as though they were born for each other, him to drink it and it to be drunk by him. This is not to say he was a chronic alcoholic – he could easily go without a drink with no fuss or negative effects – but when Darrin and beer came together there was no happier creature on God's green Earth. And it was a happiness he wanted to share.

Darrin's tireless quest to introduce me to the joys of drinking had many victories, however the piece de résistance took place on my 19th birthday, a masterclass in humiliation which, like many unfortunate events in life, can be blamed squarely on amateur theatre.

Somewhere between my political duties I had managed to co-write, co-direct and co-produce – which is to say do very little of any – a play. The play was called *Don!* and, as the exclamation mark suggests, it was a musical. The idea was to base a full-scale theatrical production on the premise that Don was quite a funny name. As it turned out the show was a smash hit, which baffled many observers – not least of whom was our family's very own Don, who couldn't see what all the fuss was about.

I was working so hard on the production that I scarcely had time to eat or sleep and so the solution, clearly, was to start taking amphetamines. In this case it was a prescription medication called Duromine that was perfectly legal – or at least would have been if I'd had a prescription for it.

The difficulty was that Duromine's prescribed use was as an appetite suppressant and given that I was six foot tall and 70 kilos soaking wet it was agreed I would struggle to convince even the most sympathetic GP of my battle with the bulge. Fortunately the proudly plump and hedonistic Liv was easily able to pop by the same doctor and come back with a bottle full of pharmaceutical-grade speed.

Being nothing if not responsible, we initially just took them in the pre-apportioned capsule form, albeit at up to eight times the prescribed dosage. But, human beings having an insatiable thirst for endeavour, we quickly discovered that by emptying the granules into a Tally-Ho paper and dropping it down our throats we could get a far more efficient rate of return on investment.

It wasn't long before my co-writer/director/producer Rohan became concerned about my sudden increase in productivity. I was running around like a dog chasing a bus until on a fateful Friday afternoon with our production chores exhausted, my jaw grinding, my pupils shrinking and my birthday looming a beleaguered Rohan suggested maybe it was time I went home and got some rest.

I wheeled inside the house in the early evening and was greeted by the hurried clatter of doors shutting and fusses being made.

Darrin intercepted me in the hallway. 'C'mon,' he said. 'I'm taking you to the pub.'

The fact that I struggled to make the 50-metre journey to the hotel on the corner did not seem to faze Darrin, who effortlessly pushed open the heavy oak door to reveal Matthew Gingold already there waiting for me. I was shuffled to the bar and Darrin made a series of vague finger gestures that the barman identified as an order for three shots of tequila and three beer chasers. Even when you were drinking something else, Darrin had always believed, there was no reason not to have a beer.

Oddly, the tequila came in tumblers instead of shot glasses but this was no great faux pas in a place where other drinks were served in plastic buckets. Darrin was laughing, Gingold was laughing, I was laughing and everything seemed to be right with the world. We ordered perhaps three or four more tequilas with the obligatory beer chasers and I was quickly ensconced in the golden glow of confidence that can only come when a man knows he is drinking responsibly in moderation.

Then Darrin grabbed my shoulder and told me it was time to go again. The two of them managed to walk me the 50 metres back home and through the front door. As I strode down the passageway I could hear some kind of fuss going on behind the door to the lounge room and was about to burst forth into it when another door on my right clicked open and a voice whispered from behind it: 'Hey Joe, come in here.'

I swayed into the bedroom and there was one of our regular houseguests, a houso lesbian drug dealer called Super Cindy whom Liv had fallen in love with for more than one obvious reason.

'I've made you a Super Cindy Special,' she said, and proffered a metal bong with half a gram of purple head packed tight into the cone. 'The trick is all about the last thumbscrew,' she explained.

I pressed the bong around my mouth, fired up the lighter and put the flame against the inch-wide cone. The brown and green turned red and then black and then disappeared down the chamber. I sucked it into my lungs, said thank you very much, and trundled back out into the hallway. There I threw open the double doors to the lounge, where I happily expected the usual household fixtures of stale pizza and Super Mario Brothers would be waiting to receive me.

But instead of the Nintendo console sitting on Darrin's favourite foam rubber chair there was a giant dining table stretching the length of the room, and sitting at it were all my housemates, best friends and even several relatives with drinks in hand and smiles blazing.

'Surprise!' they shouted in joyous unison.

'Oh,' I said, and promptly blacked out on the spot.

* * *

Darrin later said with some pride that I teetered for so long he had time to go upstairs, fetch a mattress and place it on the floor in front of me before my body finally fell flat on its face. Then he considerately dragged the mattress and the body on top of it out the back door so the rest of the party could eat their dinner undisturbed by my lifeless moans.

When I eventually came around again it was just after three o'clock in the morning, the last of the guests were leaving and my stomach felt like it was grinding quartz. I managed to stagger L-shaped back inside to discover our senior housemate Jane, a gentle and mature PhD student who had organised the whole affair, in the process of telling off Darrin for his latest transgression.

'Jesus Christ,' she said. 'I only told you to get him out of the house. I didn't tell you to get him completely shitfaced.'

'Well,' Darrin replied indignantly, 'you should have been more specific.'

Being Specific

'I told him to go to bed.'

Emma Koval, a thick-set curly-haired bisexual feminist, was explaining where her rolling drunk boyfriend Pav had disappeared to.

We were once more in the vortex of Cardigan Street, where I had settled into a chair alongside Emma and begun preparing a bucket bong. I had no interest in her and only a passing interest in the bong, but I was very interested in getting my co-editor-elect Vanessa to go to bed with me and she happened to be sitting next to both. Over the course of the evening I had ensured Vanessa maintained a steady enough intake of Carlton Draught and cannabis that by the end of it she was certain to shag the next person she saw. All that was required then was for me to be that person and so I stuck to her, as Paul Keating once so eloquently put it, like shit on a blanket.

Unfortunately, however, so did Emma Koval. Every time I tried to lure Vanessa away Emma would entrap me with a flurry of questions or, most devilish of all, ask me to play one of my latest musical compositions – a request she knew I was powerless to refuse.

I was, of course, being cockblocked, the sexual predator's most ruthlessly pragmatic pick-up technique; in fact it is so pragmatic that one of its goals is not to pick up at all. Traditional mating rituals revolve around two males competing for the affection of a female, usually by trying to capture and monopolise her attention while outperforming the rival in a show of force. Cockblocking effectively inverts this process. Instead it involves ignoring the female and monopolising the attention of the male rival, and not via a hostile contest but by pretending to strike up a friendship with them.

This presents only two possible outcomes: A) the cockblocked male eventually gets fed up with being bored to death by a stranger and departs the scene, thus leaving the female with no choice but to settle for the cockblocker; or B) the female gets so tired of being ignored she departs herself, thus escaping the cockblocker but also, more importantly, thwarting the intentions of the cockblockee. Either way the cock has been blocked, which is, after all, what the cockblock is all about.

And so as Emma Koval asked me repeatedly about what inspired me as a songwriter I marvelled at what good taste she had and thought how nice it was of her to take such an interest – no doubt Vanessa had spoken fondly of me. And when a drunk and weary Vanessa declared she was leaving I accepted it with only mild disappointment, and thanked Emma for offering to walk her home safely.

With the party now gone, I trudged upstairs to my room and noted that someone appeared to have splashed some unusually foul-smelling paint all over the walls. It wasn't until I pulled back my doona and saw the giant bald toothless man lying prone on the mattress that all the pieces came rushing into place.

In my mind I could see perfectly Pav staggering up the stairs, projectile vomiting half-digested red wine all over my room and then passing out in my bed. Then it cast back to Emma's seemingly innocent offhand remark: 'I told him to go to bed.' And then, of course, it flashed forward to Emma Koval dragging the drunken Vanessa back to her place for a night of rampaging lesbian sex.

Meanwhile I had a pale Polish socialist snoring on my pillow in a puddle of his own vomit. He had indeed gone to bed just as Emma Koval had instructed.

If only she had been more specific.

Rock Star Syndrome

If suffering through Pav's toxic expulsions was not enough to convince Vanessa of my worthiness it was uncomfortable to imagine what precisely I'd have to go through to get her over the line. There was only one thing I could think of that was more appealing to a woman than share-house living or surviving a vomit storm: I needed a rock and roll band.

Fortunately I had one – at least that month anyway. The name of the group was Miss Andry and the Boys Club, an incredibly witty concoction that only postmodern feminists could understand. Fortunately this category comprised virtually the entire population of Melbourne University arts students, which included – I did not fail to appreciate – Vanessa herself.

Even so, the name was not without its controversy. There was a school of thought that using the words 'Boys Club' in any context was inherently sexist and demeaning towards women. Further complicating matters, this school of thought resided entirely inside the mind of Matthew Gingold, who was our rhythm guitarist.

As well as possessing a commitment to academic feminism that would have put Eva Cox to shame, Gingold was a multi-instrumentalist who on top of his rhythm guitar duties liked to play bass and sing vocals from time to time. Unfortunately he was also tone deaf, and so the band found itself with both musical and ideological differences that were difficult to overcome.

Things came to a head during our debut performance at a Greens benefit at Carlton's Dan O'Connell Hotel, a gig we had managed to secure by making Matt Lennox the lead guitarist. We were not far into one of my particularly beautiful and haunting country ballads, called 'You Keep On Keeping On', when it became clear to myself and the visibly flinching audience that something was terribly wrong.

The bass guitar is the foundation stone for every chord and melodic line that brings a song to life. Fluffed solos come and go but the bass is a band's server. When it crashes, everything crashes.

To start with, every single note Gingold played was wrong, which is in itself a kind of statistical miracle. Then once he realised from my scowling that he was off key, he began frantically slapping his fingers all over the fretboard in an attempt to get back in. The result was a kind of freeform speed-jazz explosion that sounded rather out of place against the slow and gentle three-chord waltz the rest of us were playing.

In the post-mortem afterwards I angrily demanded to know what the hell had gone wrong, while Matt Lennox angrily demanded to know what the hell we were doing playing country music in the first place. As it turned out Gingold had unknowingly set his electronic tuner a semitone flat, and so when he thought the bass was perfectly in tune it was in fact perfectly tuned to be precisely out of tune with every other instrument by the most annoying possible margin known to the human ear.

But the fact remained we were all best friends and of course no one could bear to kick Gingold out of the band for one solitary human error. Instead we decided the only honourable course of action was to dissolve the group altogether and then quietly re-form it without telling him. Even for the most ardent socialist solidarity has its limits.

Over the following weeks and months we would manage to stage a couple of clandestine rehearsals and connive our way into getting the odd gig here and there. But every time Matt Gingold would find out about it and show up in the front row staring mournfully at the stage. Thus caught out we would assure him it was just a one-off event and dissolve the band again, only to re-form once more under yet another name.

And so one month we were Miss Andry and the Boys Club, the next we were Luke Warm and the Tepids, and finally we were Liv Loman and the Long Goodbyes. The beauty of this last incarnation was that Liv wasn't actually in the group, thus making Gingold feel distinctly better about the whole situation. As a result the Long Goodbyes remains the name of my band to this day, although in keeping with its heritage it has no members and has never actually played a gig.

Needless to say, it was time to pursue a solo career. And so one night I came home to Cardigan Street, unpacked my guitar and began to play.

Vital to my early success as an artist was the Cardigan Street dishes policy, a year-long cold war which dated back to an argument between Darrin and Jane over whose turn it was to do the washing up. With neither side conceding defeat and none of the other housemates wishing to get involved, an unofficial moratorium had been declared on anyone doing the dishes at all.

It did not take long for this to amass into a solid fortress of grimy and food-spattered plates and bowls and glasses piled on top of the kitchen sink, which itself had not seen daylight since the Hawke years, as well as every benchtop, stovetop and other horizontal surface available. Some housemates took to hiding their own dishes in their room, others would attempt to extract the least dirty plate they could find in a high stakes game of Jenga, while others still simply gave up using dishes altogether and lived on two-for-one chocolate bars from the local servo.

But the dishes war had one other effect: The wall-to-wall lining of crockery, glass and steel had given the kitchen the most incredible and unique acoustics I had ever experienced. You could play into the condenser mic of a tape recorder and it would come out sounding like Abbey Road.

Thus I recorded my breakthrough hit single 'Vanessa', which included such profound and cryptic lyrics as:

I long to impress her,
I just met a girl called Vanessa.

Certain I had created a masterpiece, I sent the tape to a community radio station called 3CR. I had nothing to lose: If they didn't play it, no one would hear it. If they did play it, well, no one would hear it. After all, who on Earth listens to community radio?

As it turned out the answer to that question was Emma Koval.

The First Cut is the Deepest

After such an awe-inspiring declaration of love, not to mention Emma Koval's belated imprimatur, Vanessa felt the least she could do was give me a shot. Soon we were embarking on a relationship together both as lovers and co-editors. Surely there had never been such a certain pathway to happiness.

At least some things went smoothly. After an unbeatable combination of posters, chalk and lecture-bashing, the election for the *Farrago* editorship was a foregone conclusion. We won by a factor of about two to one over our nearest rival. But what we had won now looked to be disappearing right in front of our eyes.

With the departure of the Keating government the previous year, so too had gone the federal assistance package that had topped up all the funding we'd lost under Jeff Kennett's voluntary student unionism laws. Apparently John Howard was less inclined to fund organisations whose predominant activity was holding protest marches against him and so for the first time in its history there was no money with which to run the student union, let alone the student newspaper.

Sort of, anyway. In fact once student unionism became voluntary it became our biggest selling point.

In the old days we had to justify kids being obliged to pay more than $300 a year for automatic membership of a union that most viewed with emotions ranging from indifference to hostility. The Libs were able to run a very successful line that no one should be forced to pay money to join a club which, to invoke Groucho Marx's famous conundrum, would have them as a member even if they didn't want to be one. The suggestion was that if VSU was introduced students would be able to keep their $300 and spend it on more worthwhile concerns such as, say, ten slabs of beer.

However, like almost every political line in history, this was not quite true. Even after VSU students still had to pay the $300 services fee; it was just a question of whether their money went to the university or the union. As a result when VSU came in we were able to say to incoming students, 'Hey, join the union: It's free!'

Offering free stuff to students has never been a difficult business model to prosecute and nine out of ten times they would happily sign up. And so they should have – they got countless services and endless activities, as well as free food, free beer and free concerts plus free medical attention when the latter two got out of hand.

So we kept most of the money and lost the tag of being a Stalinist forced labour camp. Meanwhile rich college kids who wanted to make a point of eschewing the union so they could continue their time-honoured traditions of shotgunning beers and hog-tying first years were free to do that too.

But as the precious few economics students in Left Focus were quick to point out, 'most of the money' is not the same as 'all of the money'. And so we soon found ourselves in an administration facing every socialist's worst nightmare: balancing a budget.

The budget of *Farrago* in particular had the arse surgically removed from its trousers, socialists always having eyed even their own media with a degree of discomfort. Any publication that didn't have the word 'manifesto' in the title was obviously cause for suspicion. As a result our wages for what was often a 24/7 job were cut to only three-quarters of those paid to other office bearers, landing at the princely sum of $300 a week – which was barely enough to cover the dope I required just to get me through layout.

Far worse was that our production budget was also monstered. Already we had gone from a weekly newspaper to a monthly magazine. Now we had a total annual budget of some $90,000 to put out ten editions of 10,000 copies each. There are Jehovah's Witness pamphlets that cost more to produce than that.

Already we paid for everything ourselves, from the petrol in the old Kingswood we made our hippie friend Ted drive for nothing, to the film in Ted's camera with which we made him take pictures – also, of course, for nothing.

The only day-to-day running cost to come from the budget was our subscription to *The Age*, *The Australian*, the *Herald Sun* and the *Financial Review*, access to newspapers being a fairly integral part of running one. However such was our newly impoverished state we couldn't even afford that anymore. Instead there could only be two. Obviously the *Financial Review* was cast aside without much regret –

it remains doubtful whether any *Farrago* editor had ever opened one – and just as obviously we all agreed that *The Age* was compulsory reading. But when it came to the two Rupert Murdoch papers we faced a Sophie's choice: Would we sacrifice *The Australian* or the *Herald Sun*?

Phip insisted that getting *The Australian* was the only responsible decision. At least it was a broadsheet, she said, and it had a strong focus on international and regional affairs – clearly vital criteria for a student publication whose entire readership existed within a two kilometre radius of Parkville.

I, however, in a rare show of forcefulness, insisted that we choose the *Herald Sun* because, to quote my exact words at the time, 'We have to know what the enemy is thinking!'

Amid all the many and terrible decisions I have ever made, I pride this one as a rare moment of clarity. Of course being a left-wing student I still considered the *Herald Sun* to be the mouthpiece of Satan himself, however I knew that even in the cash-starved ivory tower of the student union we should perhaps make the occasional effort to know what normal people were doing.

The other editors were mildly appalled but acquiesced nonetheless. After all, we had bigger, which is to say smaller, things to worry about. The $90,000 was never going to get us over the line. The absolute worst-case scenario we had accounted for was to be left with a hundred grand, which if we broke every single record for ad sales and downgraded our paper stock to tissue-thin levels might just be enough. Anything less than that and we might as well turn off the lights.

We were all scratching our heads in the office contemplating certain disaster when a call came from the general manager of the union: Someone had just donated $10,000 to the ongoing operation of *Farrago*. No strings, no conditions, just ten grand in the bank for us to do with as we pleased.

We were, naturally, perplexed. Who on Earth would donate money to a student newspaper? Certainly no one had before or since.

The answer, the GM told us, was the *Herald Sun*.

The difference between $90,000 and $100,000 was the difference between a monthly magazine and a bi-monthly one, which would have slashed our ad revenues in half. It was the difference between black and white tissue paper that would have left readers cursing at the torn pages and their ink-stained hands and newspaper-quality stock with a few pages of colour to differentiate us from every other socialist rag. It was the difference between a glossy cover that would tempt people into picking it up and a flimsy bleeding translucent smudge of washed-out shapes that share-house residents could use to wipe their arses with, as they already frequently did with the rest of the publication.

It is true that only the most sensationalist tabloid reporter could say unequivocally that without that money we wouldn't have been able to survive, however, I can say this: Without that money we wouldn't have been able to survive.

Even so, the mysterious endowment befuddled and tormented us. Obviously we immediately identified it as a cunning trap laid by the capo-fascist pigdogs trying to undermine our editorial independence, but we struggled to pinpoint precisely how they were planning to do that. After all, they'd already given us the money and hadn't even asked for a thank you. And of course there was some indignant talk that we should nobly refuse to take such blood money, but again, after much soul searching we had failed to discern exactly whose blood had been spilled. I mean here we were, a poor little newspaper taking money from a rich big newspaper. Wasn't this the redistribution of wealth we had all been fighting for?

Ultimately more powerful than any of these arguments was the one that has kept society going for millennia: Business is business and survival is survival. So we just took the money and, much like a group of childhood friends who had colluded in a grave atrocity, silently agreed to never speak of it again.

It was cause for some anxiety then, when one day we got a phone call from our mysterious benefactor inviting us to lunch with the *Herald Sun*'s editor-in-chief. Our crime had caught up with us at last – here now was the long-awaited move to cast Rupert Murdoch's evil pall over the last pure bastion of independent journalism.

'I told you we shouldn't have taken the money,' said all of us before the others could.

Angst was expressed and hands were wrung. How could we meet such a challenge with our integrity intact?

In the end I volunteered to go. After all, I was the most politically active, left-wing and morally pure member of the group. While lesser mortals might fall prey to Rupert's seductive gaze, I was incorruptible.

The Fish

I stepped out of Ted's rusted-out Kingswood and onto the freshly minted concrete of Southbank Boulevard. I was swimming in both my own sweat and a secondhand pin-striped suit. I stood up and straightened myself out as best I could while gulping down a clumsily rolled cigarette.

The editor-in-chief of the *Herald Sun* was the most powerful man to ever meet me on a voluntary basis, although to be fair his only competition at this stage was Phil Cleary. As the smoke burned my lungs I reminded myself that this was the headquarters of the evil Murdoch empire, the arch-nemesis of every red-blooded student activist. And here I was, an agent of righteousness, infiltrating its very heart.

I strode with nervous purpose into the gleaming new lobby of the *Herald and Weekly Times* headquarters by the Yarra. Before security could radio for help, I identified myself at the reception desk and soon enough an immaculately groomed young woman materialised from a lift bank and vertically escorted me from whence she came, a level so high up I felt sure the elevator would soon leave the building.

Suddenly I was standing in a boardroom surrounded by a dozen or so men and women whose suits were so sharp they could have cut wood. They were talking among themselves in low certain voices, which would here and there break into a knowing chuckle or a crisp casual profanity. All the while sunlight streamed in through a glass wall, bathing them in the sort of pure white glow normally only found at the Pond's Institute. It felt like I had stepped into a sort of corporate Olympus. So here was where the masters of the universe resided.

Upon my presence being noticed, a man sitting at the middle of the table stood up. He had carefully shorn grey-flecked hair, glasses and a plain well-proportioned face that seemed both confident and kindly. His suit was perfectly tailored to his trim and tallish frame. I decided he was the most neat and normal man I had ever seen in my life.

'Hi,' he smiled warmly, holding out his hand. 'I'm Steve Harris.'

After I'd emitted a few stumbled pleasantries he beckoned me to sit down next to him. The first 30 seconds having gone by with the most effortless grace and charm, I then proceeded to make a cunt of myself.

It began with the first plate hitting the table. It was fish, which made me involuntarily recoil in horror. My oddly indulged upbringing had left me a horrendously fussy eater but for seafood I reserved a special form of terror.

I was five years old when my father took me on a road trip to a small town called Shelley, a most magical adventure. Elevating the excitement to euphoric levels, my father asked on the way home, 'Would you like some fish and chips?'

I had always hated fish but my father, having never cooked a meal for me, had no way of knowing this.

'Yes please,' I replied, 'just without the fish.'

However somehow this message did not carry and when my father presented me with my package it contained a small piece of flake. Not wanting to display the slightest ingratitude or alert my father to his error, I picked at the chips around it.

'What's the matter?' he asked.

'Er, I just like chips,' I explained.

'Well you should've told me,' he said gruffly.

I didn't know whether he was angry at me for not liking fish, angry at himself for not knowing I didn't like fish or just angry he'd wasted 80 cents.

Either way he scrunched up the paper around the fish with unusual force and tossed it rather deliberately at the back of the shop. The rest of the drive home was somewhat less magical than the first half.

When I resurfaced back into the *Herald Sun* boardroom I saw Steve Harris curiously dividing his gaze between me and the plate of fish I was staring at. He dabbed the corners of his mouth with a napkin.

'Is everything okay?' he asked.

'Er, yes, it's fine,' I said. 'It's just that … I just … I can't eat fish.'

He paused for a moment and then looked back once more at my plate, as though it had said something to offend him.

'No problem,' he said crisply and quietly. 'We'll get you something else.'

Having bestowed such a kindness upon me, it was only fair that Steve Harris's reward be to receive a lecture on everything that was wrong with his newspaper. While the other editors and executives around him rolled their eyes, he listened patiently and carefully, inviting me to name my gripes one by one.

For a start, I said, why was the paper so pro-Kennett?

Well, he replied, so was the state. Kennett had, after all, been elected and re-elected with massive majorities.

Only 54 per cent, I countered. Yet far more than 54 per cent of his paper was devoted to the government over the opposition.

Yes, but they were the government, he said. Newspapers give more attention to governments because they're the ones in power.

But the attention was all positive, I argued.

What about the ambulance response time scandal, he replied. The *Herald Sun* had both exposed it and slammed the government for it.

Okay, I said, apart from that — what about the casino?

The casino, he noted, was Labor's idea.

Alright fair enough, I said, but what about the cuts to higher education?

That's a federal issue, he replied.

Yeah, but you backed John Howard too, I said.

Yeah we did, he said. Remember what I said about massive majorities? It's just democracy. We reflect what the people want.

But what if the people are wrong? I said.

The people are never wrong, he said. That's the whole point of a democracy.

I sat crestfallen. The real world was no place for a socialist.

'The thing is Joe,' he said. 'We're not on the Liberals' side or Labor's side. We're our own side. *You're* your own side. It's just that we're all playing the same game.'

* * *

A few minutes later I was back outside the building once more struggling to roll a cigarette, having handshaked my way from the top floor to the door. I realised I must have siphoned through at least a bottle of white wine and it had now formed a ball of fire in my empty gut and was burning up through my oesophagus until it set my whole head ablaze.

As I stood there alone, drunk and dishevelled on the immaculate footpath with the gleaming towers of Southbank all around it struck me: No one was listening to us and our little protests. But if you could get in there – *up there* – they listened. Not a thousand people chanting, just two people talking. That was the way to be heard.

I saw now that we'd been doing everything wrong – trying to tear down the system from the outside when we hadn't even understood what the system was. It was about the wrong governments winning elections because that's what people wanted. It was about newspapers ignoring oppositions because they were irrelevant and then becoming the opposition themselves when it was needed. It was where the cogs of power intersected and ground against each other, where politics and populism collided and produced their own big bang.

The system was how civilisations had risen and fallen and thrived and conquered and been destroyed in turn. It was deals and counter-deals and guts and guile and self-interest and piety and wars and diplomacy and terms of surrender. We weren't fighting it from the outside, we were part of it too – just a small annoying part that the rest of it ignored.

Now I knew how the system worked. Now I knew why Steve Harris had invited us to lunch. The truth was the system wasn't even a system, it was just life. And here we were wondering why we couldn't destroy it.

The Last Time

Throughout my editorship of *Farrago* and my relationship with Vanessa, Catherine had, to the cosmos's great relief, been on the other side of the world. But no peace is eternal other than the last.

Catherine had spent a year in Amsterdam on a student exchange program I had supportively encouraged her not to take. Naturally she had ignored this advice and somewhere in the middle of a thousand break-ups we said goodbye.

Meanwhile I had forged something resembling a life independently of her and, if not quite a man, was at least my own boy. Vanessa was a loving and decent girlfriend and I had a good and rewarding job. That should, of course, have been the end of the matter.

But if there is one thing I have learned about God it's that He never seems content to just let things lie.

When Catherine returned from Europe I felt the ground open up before her plane had even landed. Sure enough it wasn't long before she started to take an animated interest in my newfound relationship with Vanessa, to the point where she ended up inviting me to discuss it further with her in bed.

In what I felt was a particularly pointed irony, her bed was now in a large Carlton share house of the kind I had tirelessly urged her to move into when we were going out and it was only now that we had broken up she finally thought it was a good idea. Still, at last she was free of the bourgeois suburbia that had been keeping us apart.

Indeed, I noticed as she tried to kiss and cajole and coo me into yet another tryst, even the photos of her ex-boyfriends had finally gone.

However I resisted Catherine's advances that night, nobly declaring that whatever feelings for her I may have had I was still a man of honour and would never cheat on my girlfriend. The following day I resolved this impasse by telling Vanessa she was dumped.

I earnestly explained to Vanessa that I felt the rigours of our work would preclude us having a healthy and sustainable relationship and that perhaps for the good of the team it was best that we returned to being friends. Vanessa in turn pointed out that we had never actually been friends in the first place, on account of the fact that from the moment we had become running mates I had started sexually pursuing her with all the subtlety of a rabid dog. Did my sudden outbreak of professional integrity have, she wondered, anything to do with Catherine's sudden return?

Of course not, I assured her, before returning to Catherine's house later that evening.

Catherine was as wild and coquettish as ever and we talked all night in flirtatious riddles until it was time to go to bed. Lying beside her, arm in arm, I finally revealed the great news that I had ended things with Vanessa and we were free to be together again.

In an instant Catherine's limbs shrank away, almost as though they were retracting. Despite all five foot eleven of her it was remarkable how she could make herself so small.

'I'm really tired,' she said. 'Aren't you?' And with that she tugged the doona over her shoulder, turned away from me and lay there pretending to sleep until she didn't have to pretend anymore.

I lay there too in her bed, in her room, in her house. I hated her, hated being there, but I couldn't think of anywhere else to go. Treachery, after all, is a lonely calling. There was nothing left for me in this room, the air was dead and dark. Maybe there was nothing left for me in this town.

A Farewell to Arts

I had finally completed my arts degree in what I'd thought was a sprightly six years but discovered to my horror that this had not enhanced my employment prospects in the slightest. No one, it seemed, was in the market for a pretentious bong-smoking twat.

I had lost my lover, lost my politics and lost my way. My greatest achievement at *Farrago* had been a giant poster of Jeff Kennett done up as a leather-clad 1987 Michael Jackson with the words 'WHO'S BAD?' scrawled on it in mighty red letters, which I had plastered all around the city. But as I walked the streets now I saw they had all been torn down. Melbourne had moved on from me and it was time for me to move on from it.

I ended up in Tasmania for no reason other than that Liv had gone there in an ambitious attempt at clean living. When she hadn't returned for six months, Jo and I thought we'd better make sure both that she was alive and that we weren't missing out on anything, so we scraped together what little money we could and got on a plane.

Unlike everyone else I had known at uni I had never been on a plane in my adult life. Even the most incidental aspects of modern air travel were exciting and foreign to me. For example, when the hostess asked if I'd like some milk for my coffee I gratefully said that yes I would. Then when she proffered the tray for me to put my cup on I waved it away. 'Oh no thank you,' I said. 'Just the milk please.'

An hour later we marked our descent, and I saw the sweet and innocent town of Hobart gathered around the Derwent River, as though unaware of the giant mountain looming behind it. Upon arrival our luggage came to meet us on a little toy train and we managed to transfer it to one of Tasmania's three or four radio cabs and commence our journey into the city.

The first night was spent in appropriate disarray. We got drunk at a uni pub and then migrated to Hobart's only nightclub before retiring back to Liv's new place, a walk punctuated solely by the words 'Are we there ye–?' 'Oh, here it is.' Such is the economy of distance in the Island State.

The next morning we fell upon a greasy breakfast and then headed out for a walk along Sandy Bay. It was summer and our yellow star warmed the pavement and greened the grass. Even Wrest Point Casino looked unusually wholesome as it sat there watching over us in the open park below.

We were sitting in the gardens surrounding the casino, which along with the pyramids is the strongest piece of evidence that aliens once landed on Earth, when the phone rang.

The phone, an old Motorola mobile roughly the size of a small suburb, had been bequeathed to me by my mother so as to convey any urgent news from the mainland. Prior to this it had belonged to Don, however after he had been in possession of it for three months without receiving a single phone call, she persuaded him it would be put to better use in someone else's hands. Indeed, as far as anyone was aware this was the first time it had ever rung.

With some difficulty I retrieved the giant machine from my pocket, extended the aerial, flipped open the mouthpiece and answered it with some trepidation. Sure enough, it was my mother.

'You've got a call!' she gasped.

'I know Mum,' I said. 'It's you.'

'No,' she said frantically, 'a call about a job.'

'Come again?'

'You've got a job interview.'

I had never heard that sentence directed to me before in my life.

'Who was it?'

At this point my mother's excitement faded noticeably. Perplexingly, given the nature of her call, she had apparently not expected this follow-up question.

'Um, well that's the thing darling,' she said. 'I'm not quite sure.'

'Er, okay,' I said, remaining calm – a necessary skill when it came to dealing with situations my mother was involved in. 'So someone has called offering me a job but you don't know who it was?'

'Oh I know who called,' my mother retorted tartly. 'His name was John. He was lovely.'

'Great,' I said. 'John who?'

'Well, that's the part I missed.'

'I see,' I said, again with perfect equanimity. 'That's, er, okay. Where was he calling from?'

'Well I didn't quite catch that either,' my mother said in a tone that finally managed to capture the difficulty of the situation.

'Right,' I said.

'It was something-P.'

'Right, so a John P?'

'No, not John, the company. It was something-P.'

'Okay, so a word beginning with P? Like the *Daily Planet*?'

'There's no need to be like that,' she said.

'Sorry Mum,' I sighed. 'I'm just trying to figure out what the P stands for.'

'It doesn't stand for anything,' my mother said, exasperated at my stupidity. 'It was something-P. Not P for something, just P.'

I paused for a moment to process this new piece of intelligence.

'Ah, so it was two letters and the last one was P.'

'No,' she said. 'It was two letters and *then* P.'

'Okay, so it was something-*something*-P.'

'Exactly!' She paused triumphantly.

'I see,' I said. 'Now Mother, please understand that I am not being in the slightest way critical, but do you by any chance remember what the first two letters were?'

'No,' she said, deflated.

We paused together in the kind of silence our family seemed to specialise in. At times my mother's brain would just sort of freeze like a crashed computer and there was little option but to wait for it to reboot itself. Sure enough after a few seconds she sprang back to life.

'I think they were vowels if that helps.'

It did help. Shortly before leaving I had applied for a typesetting job at Oxford University Press and I reasoned that this mysterious yet lovely 'John' had perhaps been using a familiar in-house shorthand, telling my mother that he was from 'O-U-P'. I congratulated myself at having solved the mystery while trying to suppress any disappointment that the only career deemed worthy of me was adjusting the spaces in Times New Roman.

'I think I know who it was, Mum.'

'Oh that's great love!' she said. 'Let me get you the number.'

'Hang on – you've had the number the whole time?'

'Well of course,' my mother huffed. 'I'm not an idiot.'

I sat down on a park bench by the Derwent River and called the number she had just proudly dictated. There was a click and a raspy female voice crackled in at the other end.

'Something-something-P,' it said. My mother was right – for keepers of the Queen's English, Oxford University Press had some serious elocution problems.

'Er, is this Oxford University Press?'

'No.'

'Um, I mean O-U-P?'

'No, sorry darl. I think you've got the wrong number,' she said, and hung up.

And with a click all hope was gone. I sat there on the bench full of hate, directing dark thoughts towards my mother, Tasmania and the universe at large. About 20 metres away Jo and Liv were staring at me, anticipating joyous news. Now I would have to tell them that all my hinted promises of being something different, becoming something special, were just skinless balloons in the air.

I was about to pull my dead weight from the bench and deliver the news when vanity dragged me back down again to keep my dignity a moment longer. I sat there staring blankly at the big black phone, willing it to ring again. When it refused I decided to punish it by dialling the number once more.

'Something-something-P,' said the same voice. It was familiar now and I could detect the distinctive timbre of Horizon cigarettes and mixed bourbon.

'Hi,' I said. 'Is John there?'

'We've got about 50 Johns here, darl. Which one were you after?'

'Er ...' I stumbled. 'Um, sorry, what did you say the company was again?'

'Ay, Ay, *Peee*, darl,' the lady at the switch rasped.

'Did you say *A-A-P*?'

'That's right, darl,' she sighed. 'O-stray-lian *Uh*-soh-shi-ayted *Press*.'

'Holy shit,' I said.

'Come again, darl?'

'Er, sorry – um, it's about a job, I–'

'*Oh!*' she exclaimed. 'You're ringing about the cadetship.'

'Ah, I guess so.'

'Well in that case you'll be wanting to speak to John Coomber, darl. Putting you through now.'

That night I got even more drunk than usual in a share house full of sexually ambiguous Tasmanian goths and begged Jo for an airfare back home. At six o'clock the next morning I was in a taxi to the airport with my suitcase in my hand and my heart in my throat.

The Test

At seismic and unexpected moments in life, members of our family tended to make a pilgrimage to Uncle Johnny, who was universally considered to be the repository of all worldly knowledge. Having left Dandenong and moved to St Kilda, he was the closest any of us had come to interfacing successfully with the outside world.

And so upon being greeted at Melbourne Airport I was whisked to Johnny's flat to prepare me for my first foray into the professional job market.

The key part of this process involved me being fitted up in a suit whose components appeared to have been stolen from various different shaped corpses. The jacket had been made for someone a metre wide with foot long arms, such as perhaps a thalidomide baby who had later suffered from obesity, while the pants came to rest so high up my leg that they could not have safely made it to the ground without a parachute.

But impressive as they were, neither of these garments came close to rivalling the shirt, which seemed to have been designed for some as yet undiscovered species. Its elongated sleeves and tiny cuffs were more suited for tentacles than any land-based creature while its collar was so big I could've landed the plane from Tasmania on it myself.

Finally, notwithstanding my mother's distressed cries, it was decided after much heated debate that it was time for me to get a proper haircut and so I darkened the doors of a barbershop for the first time in my life.

In fairness to the barber I should stress that my unusually luscious locks have defeated many a pair of scissors and at least one emergency teacher. They were genetically predetermined to never conform to any shape nor gender acceptable to mainstream society.

Thus no sooner had the barber ceased his vigorous snipping than my hair sprang back, undefeated, into its natural state. This normally consisted of either a collection of wayward clumps or a grand unified bouffant which bestrode my scalp like a bulbous foam microphone cover. However the sum result of this haircut was that these two styles coexisted simultaneously atop a short back and sides, thus giving my head the overall appearance of a double-decker ice cream cone.

Combined with the giant-sleeved shirt and the suit whose appendages seemed to have shrunk in the wash, I looked like a doll that had been dressed by a kid with severe behavioural problems. That achieved, my mother pronounced me the handsomest man she had ever seen and packed me off to my first ever job interview.

It was late in the afternoon and the middle of summer but even so AAP's Melbourne office seemed strangely empty for a place I had figured for the beating heart of the nation's news. It later emerged that national editor John Coomber and his bureau chief Mike Hedge had already dealt with all the young hopefuls they had intended to that day and had by now decided precisely who the three lucky cadets were going to be. It was only in an act of mercy that they had decided to stay back for one last interview after a series of increasingly desperate long-distance phone calls from Hobart.

Both, no doubt, had some serious misgivings about that decision when they saw the Frankensteinian figure that walked through the door. While I had managed with some difficulty to rustle my right sleeve back enough to shake each man's hand, I then proceeded to demonstrate that I knew absolutely nothing about the company. I quickly got the sense that all three of us were wondering why we were here.

No, they sighed, AAP was not the local subsidiary of Associated Press, and no, the average story length was not 100 words, which, they explained, equated to approximately three sentences.

After I'd stammered and flubbed my way through another 20 minutes, the pair politely thanked me for my time and asked, in between glancing at their watches, if I'd like to leave some examples of my work.

I rummaged through the stack of *Farragos* I had brought — a task made unnecessarily complex by the flailing shirt cuffs flapping around my hands. Eventually I retrieved our special broadsheet edition and painstakingly unfolded the pages to access its centrespread. Carefully gripping the edge of the paper I stood up, stepped back and let it unfurl in front of me.

The next moment the two hardened newswire editors were staring at a giant poster of Jeff Kennett dressed as

Michael Jackson complete with skin-tight leather clothing and a distinctly thrusting pelvis. I then poked my head up from behind Jeff's slick black curls.

'*Who's bad?*' I said.

After a silence that made the walls ache, John Coomber was the first to speak.

'Er, you do realise that that's not exactly what we do here, right?'

'Yeah I know,' I said, defeated. 'It's pretty good though, isn't it?'

John looked at Mike, who was busy burying his fist in his mouth to stop himself from laughing. Then he looked back at me while I stood there holding an androgynous premier in my hands.

'So,' he said at length. 'Have you ever been to Sydney?'

PART III

The Yellow Sun

The Faded Emerald

I set foot on Platform One at Central Station with a broken backpack and an empty briefcase. It was somewhere around seven o'clock on a Saturday night in late March and the rains were already on their way. I sat on a bench on Eddy Avenue and smoked a cigarette while a drunk black woman pestered me for change. I gave her some and then trudged up the road to the Central Private Hotel on the peninsula between Elizabeth Street and Wentworth Avenue, one of the few places left in Surry Hills that could still call itself a genuine flea-bitten shithole. It seemed custom made for aged alcoholics and paroled sex offenders and something about the place just spoke to me.

    I did not know a soul in Sydney and so after accepting the keys from the grunting man in the cage and dumping my bags in the room I marched up to the bottom of Oxford Street and ordered a steak at Aristotle's Coffee Lounge. I had planned to sit there for a while drinking wine and smoking cigarettes while reading Manning Clarke's *History of Australia*, which my mother had assured me would bring me up to speed on what was happening around here. Unfortunately the waiter informed me that the place wasn't licensed and so I settled for a glass of lemon squash instead.

Not to be defeated, I bought a bottle of cheap white wine and took it back to my room, which, optimistically, had not one but two scratchy towels, each with a mini soap on top of them for use in the communal bathroom. Instead of a television it had a view of a dark brick wall and a moulding air-conditioning unit. With rare foresight I had thought of buying plastic cups but not a corkscrew. Undeterred I stabbed the cork in with a knife and sat there trying to focus on the events of 1788 while spitting out the occasional flotsam. Eventually the early settlers started swimming on the page and I realised there were tears in my eyes.

So, I thought. This is Sydney.

Nice Guys Finish First

At nine o'clock on Monday morning I was standing in a lift with Jim, a clean-cut boy from the suburbs, and Tom, a clean-cut boy from the country. And there was me, all shaven and shorn, with a suit and tie and a button-down shirt and a haircut that almost fit. I looked like a million bucks that belonged to somebody else.

No sooner had the two boys introduced themselves with cheerful enthusiasm than the door opened and we were all spirited through it by a friendly lady whom it was soon to emerge was our new bureau chief. She was warmer and less male than I'd imagined a hardened journo to be. In fact the whole place was suspiciously nice.

The office was a utilitarian grid of cubicles with an important-looking grown-up folded over each desk either talking into a phone or peering into a computer screen. I later discovered they had only recently replaced their old green-screen monitors with a new phenomenon called 'Windows'. This, the old timers concluded, was a dark witchcraft that would herald the end of journalism and so they stubbornly clung to their old machines until they were prised from their ink-stained hands. It was only the discovery of internet pornography that finally lessened the blow.

Sydney is nothing if not bipolar and she was as high as a kite that day. As it happened no less a personage than Queen Elizabeth II had popped in that very morning and so we had barely walked through the door when the three of us were swept up by senior correspondent Doug Conway and hustled at a trot to the Opera House steps, there to report upon Her Majesty passing by. Flushed with excitement at our first big break we were soon cantering ahead and leaving Doug in our wake.

This did not seem to trouble Doug too much, which in turn troubled me. Notwithstanding my proud anti-authoritarianism, I was still accustomed to a level of supervision roughly on the level of that offered by the Stasi. The only jobs I'd had in the real world – cold calling, delivering phone books and, for three exciting shifts, picking up empty glasses at a bar – were ones in which you were constantly monitored and one's driving professional motivation was to escape detection long enough to spend a few minutes doing nothing. But as soon as we set foot on step one of the Opera House Doug merely glanced over his shoulder to inform us he was heading straight to the accredited press area. We stuttered to a confused halt like ducklings.

'Er, what about us?' we asked.

'I dunno,' he said. 'Do some vox pops.'

Vox pops are a scientifically calibrated invention designed to keep cadets occupied and stop them getting in the way of real journalists trying to do actual work. It involves asking random strangers of no relevance to any particular story what they think about something they generally neither know nor care anything about. They are not community leaders or opinion makers or criminals or lawyers or politicians or even protesters. They are just ordinary people.

For this reason doing vox pops is the most meaningless insignificant work that a journalist can possibly do, except in the sense that it is the most important. For all the bluff and bluster of premiers and prime ministers, there is no more influential nor more elusive figure than the average punter, and the quiet unspoken rage of an elector remains democracy's most dangerous and unpredictable weapon.

The problem is the top brass of society – party leaders, ministers, CEOs, lobbyists, activists – rely almost entirely upon the so-called common person: Who they vote for, what they buy, how well they do their job. But they almost never move among them. Instead they rely on polls and KPIs and performance reviews and petitions. But to find out what people are really thinking you can't read a poll. You have to talk to them over and over again. You have to listen to them sigh and swear and shrug their shoulders and contradict themselves – all the things that can't be expressed in percentage points.

And of course to do that you have to wade through the crazy people and the nasty people and the loud ones who will never be happy. But amid them you find the normal people and the decent people, the quiet ones who sway subtly in one direction or another and cause landslides and revolutions in the process.

And so as instructed Tom, Jim and I interviewed every other person we came across on the Opera House steps,

Tom showing off his shorthand while Jim and I earnestly thrust forward our tape recorders. Each unwitting subject thus became the centre of their own mini press conference, surrounded by a flying squad of clean-cut cadets nodding in solemn agreement to everything they said. This ranged from the amicable ('I just think she's such a nice lady') to the foresightful ('It's something to tell the grandkids about') and of course the magnificently indignant: 'Well, it's the Queen isn't it? You've got to show a bit of respect.'

* * *

We returned aglow to AAP headquarters in George Street, convinced we had the story of the year – I even imagined the headline: 'MAN SHOWS RESPECT TO QUEEN' – only to find Doug already there regaling the newsroom with every detail of Her Majesty's presentation. He even noted, with somewhat unnecessary flourish I thought, that she'd been wearing the very same yellow brooch she'd been presented with on her last visit. When this was confirmed by a quick check of the archives there was an audible gasp from his audience.

'You see boys?' John Coomber said proudly. 'That's why he's the senior correspondent.'

Doug was also, we were told, the best writer at AAP, but of course that was before we came along. We gathered around our own computer terminal, scattered our notes on the desk and fumbled with the buttons on our dictaphones as we attempted to reconstruct the story of the Queen's reception. When, after 45 minutes, we had failed to come up with the first sentence, JC decided perhaps he ought to take us aside.

'Stories,' he began, 'are simple. It's just that most people have forgotten how to tell them.'

Tom, Jim and I sat listening intently, wondering if we should be writing this down.

'Remember when you were a kid?' JC said. 'Say you're coming home from school and something happens. You see a car crash or a robbery or an alien spaceship or you get bitten by a dog. So you run home and throw open the door and race up to your mum and open your mouth. What you say next – that's your lead.'

He rotated his gaze between us to see if we'd got it. Apparently we had not.

'The thing is most people try to tell a story from beginning to end. That's fine if you're writing a book but if you're writing a news story the end has to come first. The climax is the beginning.'

'Oh,' we nodded blankly.

'Okay,' said JC. 'So you see the spaceship on the way home from school. Would you say: "Mum, today we did our times tables and then we played kickball and then I got a sausage roll for lunch and then we made origami and then I was walking home with my friend Bill and then we saw a spaceship come down from the sky"?'

'Um, no?' we mumbled.

'No,' JC confirmed. 'You'd say: "Mum, there's a giant fucking spaceship outside."'

Seeing our eyes finally blink with understanding, JC went on.

'The point is that without even thinking about it the first thing you mention is the most important thing that happened. Not the first thing that happened, not everything that happened before it but the most important thing, the most unusual thing. The thing that's different and exciting and new. That's why it's called *news*. And the sentence: "I saw a spaceship on the street on the way home from school" has everything you need for a lead on a news story: Who? You. What? A spaceship. Where? On the street. When? After school. Why? Because – I dunno. Because we're not alone in the universe. Alright, forget about why. The truth is writing a story is so easy any kid could do it, kids do it every day, but for some reason not many adults can. To be honest, not even many journos can. That's why we're going to build you from the ground up. You will do news, you will do politics, you will do courts, you will do finance, you will do sport. And throughout it all you will write fast, write straight, write clean and you will put the important bits at the top. Got it?'

'Got it,' we chorused.

'Good,' he said. 'Now let's go have some champagne.'

The Dumb Question

As introductions went it was hard to beat but it left a tiny niggling hole in my brain. It seemed a straight newswire could answer who, what, when and where but not why. Was our role really only to observe and report on the world without trying to decipher the forces behind it? I couldn't help but wonder: Why *did* that spaceship land on the street? Why did I land in Sydney?

All these questions would have to wait to be answered, as all great questions patiently do. In the meantime I had to deal with the more pressing concern of day-to-day survival.

Having lasted two weeks at the Sydney Central Private Hotel without getting stabbed or molested – a statistical aberration one couldn't help but take personally – I moved to a place in East Sydney that had all the mod cons of my previous accommodation only without the congenial atmosphere.

The 'bedsit apartment' I had been so lucky to snare was a small back room on the ground floor of a three-storey 19th century boarding house. It possessed a sink and a benchtop stove, both within vomiting distance of the single bed. The bathroom upstairs was shared with the other residents and, as I discovered on my first day, several of the hookers and junkies who worked their trade from the alley at the back. It was a rare morning that I went for a shower without finding a used syringe or condom on the floor and, being a reluctant early riser at the best of times, this did little to lighten my mood for the day.

The room next door was occupied by a bisexual French backpacker whose favourite pastime was peaking out to jungle music at four o'clock in the morning and the room above was occupied by a struggling drug dealer who had some difficulty paying his debts. I learned this at 1am one night when an over-stimulated creditor bashed his door down and methodically went about smashing all his furniture while the occupant barricaded himself in the aforementioned shared bathroom, whose only desirable feature turned out to be a sturdy bolt lock. Eventually the cops arrived and hauled the redecorator away as he loudly swore to return and kill not only my neighbour but his mother and – he made a particular point of noting – his grandmother too. Not for the first time I lay in bed wondering if Sydney really was the city of my dreams.

On the day after I moved in my mother had arrived from Melbourne with several pieces of furniture in tow – Don naturally being one of them. I went to work that morning leaving behind a lone backpack on a pine single bed with a vinyl mattress and returned to find the room fully furnished with items collected from every op shop within a ten kilometre radius. This included a double bed Don had managed to strap to the roof of the car and navigate back through the narrow streets of inner Sydney by sticking his head out the window, a feat that made his eyes water even in the retelling. The various furnishings were then bedecked in old bedspreads and tablecloths and towels my mother had brought up with her until it resembled any other room in our old house back in Dandenong.

But once she'd left a few days later it was back to me against the world and the world was still Sydney, this strange, loud and violent town that was less a vibrant metropolis than a constant guerrilla attack. Seeking refuge, and undistracted by anything resembling a social life, I plunged myself into AAP. The only thing I embraced more enthusiastically than the work was the after-work drinks and the forestalling of my inevitable return to that strange and solitary chamber.

The result of this sorry desperation was that I quickly became known as a willing friend to anyone who felt the need for a cold beer at the end of a hard day. I gained a solid reputation for working hard and late, even when I was just seeking camaraderie or waiting for the next round of shifts to finish in the hope that it would deliver me a drinking partner and thus somebody to talk to. Somewhere amid this quiet halfway time at the office, combing through websites and transcripts, and the incidental tips and tidbits I picked up from old beer-soaked journos at the pub, I gradually pieced together some vague idea of what my job description was.

In between these nights were the days themselves. The press conferences where I was too timid to ask a question; the stakeouts where residents or police officers would brush past my squeaks without comment; the court cases where I struggled to identify the victims from the criminals or even the law that was supposedly broken. Every morning I was dropped into something completely new, each day a different scene that was surreal or scary or a moment in history. There was no greater job in the world, and no person less qualified to do it.

The one golden rule of journalism I have since come to live by is this: Always ask the dumb questions. If you don't know something, ask. If you still don't understand it, ask again. Yet sadly I was too dumb to even do that. Instead, like most dumb people, I thought I was smart.

And so rather than seeking answers from politicians that might produce a trip-up or at least some information I would get into arguments with them that produced precisely nothing. Rather than asking cops to explain a crime in English instead of police bureaucratese, I would nod knowingly at their jargon, only to realise halfway through filing my story that I had no idea what had actually happened.

I finally learned my lesson at a federal police press conference about a drug seizure from a shipping container full of whitegoods. The ecstasy tablets were bagged up in their thousands and the fridges that once hid them were likewise on proud display. While the real police reporters rattled through times and dates and numbers, I noticed that the fridges had strange black marks on them. Still dumb enough to think I was smart I thought I had picked the vital clue.

'Um,' I said to the senior inspector, 'those black marks on the refrigerators. Is that what tipped you off?'

'Er, no,' said the officer. 'That's our fingerprinting dust.'

The old cop reporters all rolled their eyes and said, 'Corrr ...' while a few newly enlightened cadets at the back went 'Ahhh ...'

Stupidity had finally caught up with me. At last I had mustered up the dumb question and while I was humiliated in front of a few grizzled old warhorses I was also saved from humiliating myself in front of every reader that read the story and newspaper that read the wire. It was the best question I'd ever asked.

The Bear Pit

Despite such heroic efforts in fighting crime, my true love was still always politics and after a few years at Australian Associated Press I eventually became the state political correspondent. This was a position as enthusiastically venerated by AAP as it was enthusiastically ignored by everybody else, not least the politicians themselves but that was fine by me. I'd just come along for the show.

Labor was in government and the Honourable Bob Carr was premier of NSW. Whether in parliament, in a press conference or ordering an egg-white omelette he was without doubt the greatest political performer of his generation. It is testimony to Carr's incredible charisma and skill that in the largest and most brutal political sphere in the country he lasted almost a decade as opposition leader and another decade as premier with barely a sniff of a challenge from any contender from his side of politics or the other. It was only after he had been retired for a year or so that everybody looked around at each other with tousled hair and the faint craving for a cigarette and realised he hadn't actually done that much.

Carr's great strength was an intense combination of intellect and vanity that rendered him invulnerable to all combatants. When ordinary people succumb to pride they usually end up dead in gunfights or boating accidents but Carr's unassailable sense of self-worth was almost clinical. Unlike many leaders, he was convinced of his own supremacy not because he was deluded or psychopathic but because his mighty brain had calculated his own value against everybody else's and reluctantly come to the conclusion that he was indeed the greatest of them all.

Carr did to Labor politics what Michael Jordan did to basketball: He changed the way it was played. Whereas premiers before and since had been beholden to the party machine in Sussex Street or the factional warlords in caucus, Carr was able to deftly avoid their grasp as surely as the Roman general whose society he was a member of. Just as Fabius Maximus had averted catastrophe for Rome by ducking and weaving and gradually exhausting the armies of Hannibal, Carr challenged the Labor orthodoxy without ever engaging it in a pitched battle from which he could not retreat to safety. A typical example was his effort to privatise electricity supply in 1997, a move that would have brought now unimaginable riches to the impoverished burghers of NSW. Carr pushed hard for the sale but only on the condition it was backed by Labor Conference – a mandate that would have hog-tied any pesky unions who tried to campaign against it later. However when the motion was voted down by delegates he not only solemnly vowed to abide by Conference's decision, but went out and won the next election on an anti-privatisation platform, thus positioning himself as a champion of democracy. Any student of politics seeking to learn how to turn a defeat into victory need look no further than that.

Indeed, in a neat illumination of Carr's dexterity, when his successor Morris Iemma attempted an almost identical move a decade later he was summarily executed within weeks. Iemma had fought a heavyweight bout with his fists. Carr always knew the real trick was to move your feet.

As well as taking on the party, Carr was also a master of the art of waging Fabian war against his own administration. He painted himself not just as the leader of his government but also as the leader of any opposition against it, thus rendering the actual opposition redundant. If the electorate was angry, he was *furious*. If, in the course of some particular scandal, the Liberals demanded the sacking of a senior bureaucrat, Carr sacked the director-general. Eventually he even sacked Eddie Obeid, perhaps his greatest service to the people of NSW.

Carr treated Liberal attacks like they were mosquito bites while subsequent state and federal Labor governments succumbed to them as though they were malaria. In the dying days of the Gillard government Labor strategists attempted to cast the Prime Minister as the victim, but far from garnering sympathy it merely cost her authority. Carr's pride, let alone his political nous, could never countenance that. He would never allow himself to be seen as besieged by the opposition. As far as he was concerned they weren't even in the same fight. In one memorable parliamentary performance he responded to a question from the opposition benches simply by saying the word 'No' in 26 different languages – including, just for the hell of it, Eskimo.

But it was the press conference that was Carr's favourite theatre of war, and thus the attempts by the press gallery to wrong-foot him required increasingly desperate and imaginative lines of attack. And so during an otherwise pedestrian reannouncement about the state's motion picture industry, I decided it was the perfect opportunity to ask him a question about paedophilia.

For reasons that defy any earthly explanation, at the height of my AAP days I had taken to wearing a torn corduroy jacket to work. This item of clothing was the last keepsake of my relationship with Catherine, which is to say, as the right-over-left buttoning system attested, I had stolen it from her. Fortunately, lest anyone consider this practice too effeminate, I had also grown a long wispy beard whose chin-warming powers I augmented with a ragged woollen scarf. The only drawback of this magnificent ensemble was that if I stood too long in the one place people started throwing change at me.

Thus adorned, I presented myself amid the media scrum at Haymarket's Capitol Theatre, where Carr was holding his press conference about film production tax breaks. However the story of the day was that a former federal Labor MP from the Northern Territory called Bob Collins was facing multiple child sex offences. There was a feeling among the journos that a question had to be asked but no one had the courage, nor the faintest idea of how to draw the connection given that the two men could not have been further removed from one another in time, space or inclination.

As Carr's minders were calling for last questions a supposed friend in the press gallery whispered in my ear, 'I dare you to get a question up.'

The very prospect of this left my underpants in grave danger of losing their status as the only clean item of clothing I was wearing. But a dare was a dare.

'Er, no problem,' I said, and cleared my throat. 'Um, Premier?'

'Yes?' He beamed a cool electrical gaze.

'You're, uh, the most senior serving leader of the Labor Party in government at the moment ...'

'I am,' he replied, as though reciting lines in a marriage ceremony.

'Er, do you have any words of advice for the paedophile Labor MP Bob Collins?'

Carr shot me a glance that could've killed a moose at a hundred yards. Then he paused for what seemed like several years and tapped his already immaculately aligned briefing notes on the rostrum.

'You know,' he said at length, 'ever since you started dressing like a character out of Dostoyevsky your questions have become more interesting.'

The breath-baited media pack laughed uproariously on cue.

'And,' he added, 'more stupid.'

Therein lay the difference between a Labor scandal and a Carr scandal, namely that the latter generally failed to materialise. A lesser politician would, with ample justification, have summoned a righteous indignation and publicly denounced the disgraceful and outrageous nature of the question. In the more toxic phases of the Gillard government it might even have been grounds for a media inquiry. But Carr just casually batted me away like an insect and killed the issue dead with one stroke.

As the rest of the pack dispersed, Carr leaned in towards me as he walked towards the door.

'You idiot,' he grinned. 'Did you really think I was ever going to answer that?'

For a less-assured government it could've been the Cuban Missile Crisis but for Bob it was just another quiet day at the office. So many unnecessary wars are averted when just one person doesn't lose their shit.

Picking Winners

Perhaps the greatest indicator of my early news judgment and political acumen was the James Hardie asbestos saga, the greatest corporate and industrial outrage to engulf Australian society since World War II. A company had left thousands of employees prone to a deadly disease and then fled offshore, leaving countless workers stranded without hope of justice or compensation. And I was there when it all began.

The fax came through to the AAP office at NSW Parliament House. The State Government was to launch a Special Commission of Inquiry into Hardie's unconscionable conduct and whether it had deliberately underfunded its compensation scheme, thus abandoning thousands of dying workers. The fuse had been lit and Australia's biggest ever corporate scandal was about to explode.

I filed the story as a brief.

This is not to say I wasn't diligent in my journalistic duties. Of course I called James Hardie for a response but I was assured by their spokesperson that this was nothing out of the ordinary and nothing to do with James Hardie anyway given that the company responsible for compensation was a little known acronym with no legal ties to its former parent. It was nothing more than a placenta and the umbilical cord had been cut, although I don't think the spokesperson put it in precisely those terms.

Luckily a good journalist can penetrate through such spin and obfuscation but unfortunately there wasn't one around. I filed James Hardie's response as a second brief and prepared to leave the office.

Another slow news day, I thought.

* * *

The basic skills of journalism having obviously eluded me, I did what every failed reporter tries to do and set out to become a columnist.

While AAP frowned upon anything resembling an opinion, as the NSW political correspondent I was allowed to write a 'news analysis' each Friday that attempted to decode the week's events. The rules were clear: I was permitted to analyse things, as the name suggested, and perhaps, if the subs were in a generous mood, even interpret them. But under no circumstances could I ever say what I thought about them.

For a young man of my particular disposition this obviously presented some challenges. The pieces began tamely enough, and were even regarded by some of the lesser informed members of the press gallery as insightful, but soon the inevitable happened. There are few forces in nature strong enough to keep an opinion away from a keyboard.

Late one Friday afternoon, my heart joyous with the prospect of work drinks just minutes away, I stood next to

John Coomber's desk while he read that week's masterpiece, which was brutally excoriating one of Carr's ministers for a crime so mild it now eludes me. I peered over his shoulder directing him to various passages of great wit and insight as though I had just delivered him Watergate.

'So, do you love it?' I asked.

JC dragged a reluctant cloud of air through his teeth.

'I hate it,' he replied.

My mind and body deflated as one. 'But ... But why? It's right isn't it?'

'It doesn't matter whether it's right or not,' he said. 'It's opinion. And that's not what we do here.'

'It's not opinion, it's analysis,' I protested.

'You say the guy should be sacked.'

'Yeah. Well, er, that's my analysis.'

'No, that's not analysis. That's an opinion. We're a newswire. We report the facts. We don't report what the facts should be.'

'But that's the conclusion,' I said. 'How can you analyse something without reaching a conclusion?'

'A conclusion comes down on one side or the other. We report it straight. Both sides. Balanced.'

'But what if one side's wrong? Isn't it our job to tell people what's right?'

'No,' JC replied. 'It's not our job at all. If you want to write like that you should go and join a newspaper.'

He briefly scanned my face with his gentle grey eyes and then went back to studying the wire.

The Knowledge

A little while ago a visiting American on a work trip called me from his hotel and asked me how long it took to get to Holt Street. I told him '15 minutes'. I should have said 28 years.

News Limited's Surry Hills headquarters was just a few minutes from the CBD, 800 kilometres from Melbourne and a million miles from home. My mother was the sort of person who carried around a bumper sticker in her purse that said 'Murdoch Lies'. The comrades who I'd rallied with at uni would, had they ever met Rupert Murdoch, have started fossicking around for an improvised explosive device.

'Oh,' my mother said when I told her I'd got the job. 'Well I *guess* I'm happy for you ...'

I was hired by the then-editor of *The Daily Telegraph* Campbell Reid on the advice of the opinion editor David Penberthy but despite this both men still hold senior positions at the company.

The interview itself was a fairly cursory affair. Penbo, Campbell and a couple of other senior staffers sat in the editor's office to survey the crumpled and bearded creature before them. True, while escorting me up Penbo had noted with surprise that I had bothered to put on a tie, but unfortunately it was not the best tie in the world. It wasn't even the best tie in the elevator.

In tall tales told at the *Tele*'s old drinking grounds it was later said that one of the more observant attendees at the interview remarked after my departure, 'He seems like a bit of a fuckwit,' to which another had thoughtfully mused in response: 'The question isn't whether he's a fuckwit. The question is whether he's our kind of fuckwit.'

Finally I had found a job description I could relate to.

* * *

I joined the *Telegraph* as the workplace reporter, which had recently been rebranded 'Work and Family Reporter'. While I was well versed in the union movement and industrial relations, it would be fair to say community concern about childcare shortages and Family Tax Benefit A were not acutely felt by a single 28-year-old chain-smoking alcoholic. Nonetheless I tried my best and was staggered to learn that workplace issues did not end at the workplace. Hell, once you covered work and family there wasn't much left. Work and family was life, or most people's lives anyway, which was another thing I didn't know much about.

The problem was that things that were normal to most people – be it a car unadorned with folk murals, an item of clothing that the previous owner hadn't died in or a toilet that didn't require basic survival skills – were unknown to me while I was growing up. Meanwhile the people I'd met at university were the children of wealthy professionals, and if they ever wore secondhand clothes they did so largely to prove they were socialists.

I had gone from being a freak surrounded by poor people to a freak surrounded by rich people. While my mother delivered her sermons about a life of impossible piety and my comrades had preached confidently of the revolution to come, somewhere above and underneath and around it all was a certain demographic I had never really thought to consider: everybody else.

Or, for want of a better description, *Daily Telegraph* readers.

The notion that people who read the *Tele* are a single mass of seething right-wing racists or drooling slavish zombies is as stupid as it is snobbish. Certainly it is a paper read by extremists and crazies but that is only because it is a paper read by everybody – including, apparently, the extremists and crazies on the other side who abuse it. That ten per cent jump up and down and get excited about something and might write letters or comments or broadcast arguments in the pub that are by turns wild or hilarious or abusive or, to put it diplomatically, somewhat eccentric. They are often the most entertaining but they are not most people.

On a good day a million people pick up the paper and flick through it and 90 per cent of them put it down having got their news fix or racing tips or footy results and they never say another word. They call them the silent majority for a reason.

* * *

The first story I got for the paper was about how the Labor Council was changing its name to Unions NSW. It was a seemingly innocuous move that was in keeping with the regrettable tendency of all organisations to abandon their historical roots and rebrand themselves with a soulless new font and moniker that would both catapult them into the modern age and ditch all grammatical pretence in one fell swoop. There was also the fact that NSW was now residing under an aged Labor government which, even under the magic of Bob Carr's Oscar-worthy performances, was increasingly on the nose.

The story was handed to me as a welcoming gift by a man who knew the trauma of being a new storyless reporter on the *Telegraph*, having worked there himself in my exact role. He'd since become the communications director for the Labor Council, whose rebranding, like many other efforts to drag the Labor movement kicking and screaming into the 21st century, was his idea.

I duly filed the piece in straight up and down AAP style and after a solid ten hours crammed with coffees, meetings, desperate phone calls begging for yarns, three hours of computer training and another three hours trying to find a computer, I figured I would leave for the day.

I was ordering a hamburger at a greasy take-away joint in Oxford Street at about 8pm when my mobile rang. It was a call from the backbench, the penultimate layer of newspaper production where good stories go to live or die.

'Mate we need a breakout comment to go with the union yarn – about 15 cems should do it,' an anonymous voice said.

The sentence contained at least two words I didn't

understand and unfortunately they seemed to be the important ones. 'Er, okay,' I said. 'When do you need it?'

'Twenty minutes will be fine mate.'

'Ah, sure. How should I get it to you?'

'Shit mate, I dunno. How about using a fucking computer?'

I looked around. The Olympic Yeeros and Pizza Bar didn't appear to have a computer as far as I could see, although there was a tempting selection of potato cakes in the bain marie which distracted me briefly.

'Um, yeah. No worries,' I said.

'Alright. Jesus, it's only 15 cems.'

'Um, okay. How long is that?'

There was a pause on the other end of the line. 'Ah, it's 15 cems.'

The caller hung up and the potato cakes looked at me helplessly.

I did not have a computer but fortunately I had a girlfriend, and fortunately that girlfriend had a sister, and fortunately that sister had a computer. I went to their house and 15 minutes later I'd bashed out 250 words. Then I ran to an internet café and emailed them to the office with minutes to spare.

'Did you get that?' I asked anxiously on the phone.

'Nah, you missed deadline,' said the voice. 'But we'll get it in for the second.'

It was 9pm when I finally managed to have my first beer after day one on the job.

'Geez,' said my girlfriend. 'Is it always gonna be like that?'

'Nah,' I replied, swallowing half a cigarette. 'I'm sure it was just a one-off.'

The next day I came into work to find my story spread across the top of page three beneath the screaming headline 'UNIONS NAME THE PROBLEM: IT'S LABOR'. I dropped my coffee and my jaw.

That moment the phone rang and sure enough it was my friend from the Labor Council. I braced myself for a blast through the receiver.

'Mate!' he said.

'I know,' I said. 'Sorry.'

'Sorry? What the fuck are you sorry for? That was the best run ever. I love it.'

'What about the bit that says you guys are trying to shaft the Labor government?'

'Well we are.'

'But you told me you couldn't say that.'

'Of course I can't say it but *you* can. Jesus, someone has to.'

Breaking News

My friend was right. At AAP I had frequently clashed with the editors because I wanted to break news instead of just reporting it, an ambition only slightly compromised by the fact that I didn't really know how to. Even when I got my first big scoop back at AAP it was someone else's.

This was the infamous 'Stolen Wages' scandal, which was uncovered by Chris Graham of the *National Indigenous Times*, a fine and appropriately crazed journalist who pursued Aboriginal issues with enough angry righteousness to power a nuclear reactor.

In this case he'd discovered that the NSW government was withholding – or, to be more specific, had accidentally misplaced – up to $70 million it was supposed to have kept in trust for lowly paid Aboriginal workers. As it happened this discovery took place just when the Howard government was under extreme pressure to apologise to the Stolen Generation. Now it emerged that governments hadn't just stolen the children of Aborigines, they'd stolen their money as well. It was both a great moral outrage and a ball-tearer of a yarn.

But Chris didn't just want bragging rights, he needed the state government to be pressured into handing over the dough. And the problem was, as he knew from bitter experience, that governments tended not to cave in to whatever the *National Indigenous Times* had to say. And so when he wanted a really big hit he would seek out a top journalist on a big metro paper and get them to plaster the story on the front page.

None of this, however, explains why he came to me. And such was Chris's paranoia about revealing sources that he never told me who it was that advised him the best way to get his biggest scoop to date on the front page of a newspaper was a hapless state political reporter who didn't even work for one.

And so, fresh off a plane from one of Bob Carr's Byron Bay charm offensives, I went to meet the originator of a mysterious phone call at a coffee shop near Parliament House. I'd expected to be confronted by an angrier version of Aden Ridgeway but instead found myself sitting across from a burly shaved-headed white man in a T-shirt and jeans. He was certainly like no political journalist I'd ever seen. Rather, he looked like he'd just come from a war zone and as far as he was concerned he had.

After a brief handshake and exchange of our credentials – he had plenty, I had none – Chris produced his smoking gun: a 2001 Cabinet minute that detailed the government's liability but which had, in the three years since, been buried or at least conveniently forgotten about. It was the most exciting document I had ever seen and he waved it like a weapon but when I went to take it he reflexively pulled it back, like Frodo Baggins with a certain ring. I could see it, he said, but I couldn't have it – he didn't like me even touching it.

With rare diplomacy I asked if I could at least take notes, a request to which Chris graciously acceded and then watched with increasing anxiety as I proceeded to transcribe the entire document into my agonisingly slow shorthand. Eventually I got the material I needed and, thanks to Chris's patient and repeated explanations, some remote understanding as to what it all meant. It was a Friday afternoon and the shadows were lengthening over the Domain. We agreed that I would put the story on the wire the following Monday and at last the public would know.

The only catch was that the wire didn't go to the public, it went to other journos and editors; whether they picked the story up and actually put it in the paper was entirely out of my hands. Indeed whether they even noticed it would be a coin toss at best. So there I was in the fading light assuring Chris Graham that he had chosen the right vessel for his warhead and that his story would deliver justice for the families of some 11,500 Aboriginal people and rock the government. And this from someone who couldn't even rock the Dan O'Connell Hotel.

And even if a major paper did run a wire story they would almost never run it on the front page. The only exceptions were during a journo strike or when a particularly passive-aggressive editor wanted to send an angry message to his reporters that they had all failed that day. Splashing on a yarn you didn't break was the greatest mark of shame for any self-respecting masthead.

So on the Monday morning I called in my friend Nick O'Malley from the *Sydney Morning Herald* and told him a big story would hit the wire that day. But, I assured him, it would not be until after 6pm and it would carry no bells.

This would make it too late for radio and television and virtually guarantee it went unnoticed by the other papers. All he had to do was wait for me to tell him it was sent and the *Herald* would have a page one scoop. O'Malley asked me what the story was and I told him.

'Shit, that *is* a good yarn,' he said. 'I take it you got it from someone else?'

The next day the Stolen Wages scandal was splashed across the front page of the *Herald* – or at least across three square inches of it. Still, it was a page one story and that was all that mattered. In March 2004 the NSW government apologised to the victims and their descendants and announced the long-awaited compensation scheme. That year Chris Graham, myself and another *National Indigenous Times* reporter were highly commended at the Walkley Awards, which was a polite way of them telling us we'd come second. Clearly, much like the subjects of the story itself, we were robbed.

I pretty much gave up on entering the Walkleys after that, however I was subsequently invited to judge the awards in various categories – a role in which I took great delight. Sure, it was hard to select three finalists or one winner from a stuffed cardboard box full of entries but the joy of depriving the dozens of losers more than made up for it.

None of this mattered though – I had tasted blood. For the first time I realised that the right story in the right place could be a powerful agent for change – sometimes even for the better. Over the next six months at AAP I spent more and more time trying to break big yarns and less and less on reporting the news of the day, much to the frustration of my long-suffering bureau chief. By the time the *Telegraph* asked to see my CV I could proudly present them with three major scoops I had broken in that year alone. It wasn't until I started working there that I discovered the expected output was one a day.

And so I threw myself into the workplace round like a turd at a fan, meeting every single union leader, every minister and opposition spokesperson, every industrial law firm and every employer group, every disgruntled worker or angry boss I could find. The speech was always the same: Each of them had to come to me first with anything new – anything that happened, big or small. I handed out my number like a carpet-cleaning flyer and to make my point I even broke the journalist's most sacred covenant by paying for the beers and coffees myself. Well, sometimes anyway.

Either my financial outlay or my desperation paid off. Soon I was the primary port of call for just about every work-related story to hit the public domain and if I ever missed one I at least heard about it first from a source ringing to apologise. News is a hard business and there is no better instinct in any journo than being shit-scared of missing a yarn – a fact the *Tele*'s editors knew only too well. When it happened at AAP shoulders would be shrugged and a few paragraphs hurriedly sent out on the wire. When it happened at the *Telegraph* pools of liquid would form under the reporter's feet.

As a result of this motivational fear I usually managed to get one, two or three page leads in the paper each day – a strike here, a sexual harassment case there and a childcare scandal in between – but after several months at the paper page one still eluded me. It seemed that no story in industrial relations could muster the ingredients of a bona fide splash.

And then one day, as the rest of the world was going about its business, somebody declared they were going to hire a sniper to kill Multiplex crane drivers unless the company paid him $50 million.

Even I could see there might be a yarn in that.

Multiplexity

One could be forgiven for thinking that a crazed blackmailer threatening to use a sniper to kill crane drivers unless he was delivered a briefcase-sized sum of money was already as good as a story could get but there was even more. The anonymous extortionist also demanded that the company only contact them via secret messages planted in a newspaper. It was like an episode of the *A-Team* except without the fine production values.

The story spread like an epidemic across Australia and then to the UK, where a similar threat was made to Multiplex over the redevelopment of Wembley Stadium. Soon it was all over the world. A host of the usual colourful characters were swept up in the speculation, including known underworld identities and the obligatory former boxer, but all denied any involvement and the blackmailer's identity remained a mystery.

My chief of staff at the time was a precociously intelligent young power freak called John Rolfe, who, as God had apparently ordained for all my instructors, looked uncannily like my father. If Danny Bertossa had sculpted his facial hair and got a short back and sides they could have been exactly the same person. Indeed, I had no evidence to suggest that they weren't.

Rolfey handed me a copy of a classified ad found in the 19 February 2005 edition of *The Weekend Australian* which he had identified as being slightly unusual, largely on the grounds that it read as follows:

svgucsk bfptat nskweum ds mz yxtqa – lv@jxplbgzcj.vts

'I think it's him,' he said.

At this point the theme tune from *Mission: Impossible* should've started playing but instead all I heard was the siren song of the Mad Scientists Club.

'I'll get to work on it immediately,' I said.

Rolfey's immaculately groomed face contorted into a shape I had come to recognise in many of my superiors, being a combination of stark confusion and mild annoyance.

'Um, what do you mean?' he asked.

'I mean I'll get started on it straight away. I know it's late but I'm happy to work back.'

'Jesus,' Rolfey laughed. 'We don't want you to solve it. Just write a story about it.'

I obediently filed what is known as 'a strong downpager' – a strange mid-range story halfway between a page lead and a brief – and packed up for the day, taking great care to stuff the crumpled coded message into my bag.

What neither the Multiplex extortionist nor Rolfey had counted on was that both my grandfather and my father had trained me in the art of cryptic crosswords from a grossly inappropriate young age. Indeed, my father was known to withstand up to 45 minutes in our outside toilet quietly wrestling with the things – a fact his youthful doppelganger should surely have been across.

Moreover I was intimately familiar with the work of a child detective called Encyclopedia Brown, whose youthful exploits were the inspiration for my own Hildebrand Detective Agency – a shortlived enterprise headquartered in the tool shed next door to my father's favourite place of respite. And on top of this I of course had my Mad Scientist training, should a drain need unblocking along the way. Needless to say I felt I was more than a match for the word games of a vengeful mobster.

And yet after hours of staring at the code throughout the night I still couldn't crack it. Even the twelve beers I had did little to improve my clarity.

I arrived at work the next morning a thoroughly defeated and slightly hungover man. And so I did what all desperate journos do: I turned to Google.

To start with I typed in the word 'codes', which produced some impressive results, namely 764 million of them. Clearly I was going to have to refine my search somewhat.

And so I searched for alphabet codes and then numerical codes and then alphanumeric codes and then something called the Caesar code and on and on until I found myself drowning in a whirlpool of letters and numbers that made no sense to each other, let alone to me, and certainly seemed far from the nonsensical jumble of improbably high-scoring Scrabble words this goddamn sniper was laying down on the board.

It was five o'clock and I was just about to get some lunch when I came across something called the 'Vigenere cipher'. Suddenly, to use a term befitting the world wide web, something clicked.

A certain type of Vigenere code involves a keyword that is needed to transform one set of letters into another, which it does by running that keyword repeatedly over a message. The problem was that I couldn't get the original message without the keyword, and to get the keyword I had to figure out what the original message was. In other words I had to solve it backwards.

It helps if you think of it like a ham sandwich. The top layer of bread is the message someone is trying to send and the bottom layer is the gobbledy-gook that arrives. The keyword that unlocks them is the ham.

To get each letter in the keyword, you have to measure the alphabetical distance between each letter in the original message – i.e. what they are trying to tell you – and its corresponding letter in the encrypted message – i.e. the jumbled letters you are looking at. Then you measure the distance in number between the letter in the original and the letter in the code. Then you count out that numerical value from the beginning of the alphabet and that gives you the corresponding letter in the keyword.

To get started it is helpful to number each letter of the alphabet like so:

1	2	3	4	5	6	7	8	9	10	11	12	13	14
A	B	C	D	E	F	G	H	I	J	K	L	M	N

15	16	17	18	19	20	21	22	23	24	25	26
O	P	Q	R	S	T	U	V	W	X	Y	Z

So here was what I had in front of me:

SVGUCSK BFPTAT NSKWEUM DS MZ YXTQA – LV@JXPLBGZCJ.VTS

The last bunch of letters obviously looked like an email address, so I guessed that .VTS was .COM. By counting the letters between VTS and COM and then counting that number from the beginning of the alphabet I should have got the three letters of the keyword in between but the letters were as random as the code itself. I then tried it using GOV and ORG – even EDU in case I was dealing with a disgruntled university professor. None of them worked. The sequence of letters they produced simply didn't exist in any word in the English language I'd ever come across.

It wasn't until I had checked the Multiplex website for the thousandth time that I noticed their web address was www.multiplex.biz. Suddenly the Holy Grail sang to me. So this was how it worked:

BIZ   original message
???   unknown keyword
VTS   encoded message

Counting from the Z (26) in the original to the S (19) in the code, running through the alphabet like an unbroken loop and including both letters in the count, the numerical distance was 20. That then meant the letter in the keyword was the 20th letter of the alphabet, namely T. Thus it was revealed: ULT was part of the keyword.

Finally I had a sequence of letters that could at least belong in a word, and a word I figured I could guess at. Soon the keyword's rather sinister character revealed itself:

MULTIPLEX.BIZ – original message
XDESTROYM.ULT – keyword
JXPLBGZCJ.VTS – encoded message

The keyword, clearly, was 'DESTROY MULTIPLEX'. For all the cloak and dagger intrigue it seemed our extortionist was about as subtle as Darth Vader.

Having cracked the keyword it wasn't long until I had the lot:

PROBLEM PLEASE CONTACT ME ON EMAIL – AR@MULTIPLEX.BIZ

As it turned out it wasn't the extortionist after all. It was someone inside Multiplex sending a message to the extortionist. Maybe he was trying to buy time, maybe he was trying to flush out a traceable email or IP address or maybe – and not implausibly given what was obviously a difficult few days at the office – he was just experiencing a genuine problem. And that person was none other than Multiplex CEO and owner Andrew Roberts.

* * *

It was a modest six o'clock in the evening when Rolfey came past my desk again to find me peering at scattered pieces of paper, furiously counting up and down the random letters and numbers I had scrawled on them. It was a wonder he didn't call HR.

'Don't tell me …' he said.

'It's okay,' I replied. 'I've finished now.'

'Good,' he said. 'Go home.'

'Actually I think you should see this,' I said, and handed him a small torn sheet.

'What's this?' he asked.

'That,' I said, 'is your message.'

Splash

To Rolfey's great credit he was never slow to pick up on things.

'Holy shit,' he said solemnly. 'You'd better come with me.'

He dragged me across the newsroom floor and presented me at the door of the editor's office where Campbell and Penbo were debating what to put on page one.

'Tell them,' he said.

Campbell and Penbo stopped talking and raised two pairs of eyebrows in my direction.

'I cracked the code,' I said.

'Bullshit!' said Penbo.

I handed him the piece of paper. 'That's the message.'

Penbo appraised it carefully. '"Problem. Please contact me." Pretty fucking boring message for a criminal mastermind.'

'It's not him. It's someone inside the company contacting the blackmailer, just like he'd instructed them to.'

Campbell had now taken the piece of paper and was studying it.

'Er, how exactly did you do this?'

'Well apparently it's something called a Vigenere code and it can't be cracked without a special keyword but you can't get the keyword unless you know what the original message is which is obviously a bit paradoxical but anyway I figured—'

'Hang on,' Penbo cut in. 'What was the keyword?'

'Er, "Destroy Multiplex".'

'Now that's pretty fucking good,' Penbo said. He looked at Campbell with dark earnest eyes. 'We should splash on that.'

Campbell rocked back in his chair and drummed his fingers together the way I'd always hoped editors did.

'Hmmm,' he said. 'It's good alright. Definitely a page three but I'm not sure if it's enough for the splash. It's just too narrow. We need something that will broaden it out, something that will make everyone care.'

'Oh come on,' Rolfey said gallantly. 'The bloke even proved me wrong. That's a splash in itself.'

Campbell sat surveying us, like a firm but fair father in a 1950s sitcom. 'Let me think,' he said. 'What did you say the name of the code was again?'

'Ah, Vigenere,' I said. 'Um, I think it's like *Vigg*-ner? or maybe Vie-*genner*?'

'Jesus Christ!' Campbell spun his chair around and dived into his computer, tapping wildly. 'It's *visionaire*!' he cried. 'It's pronounced *visionaire*! I read about it somewhere. In fact I think ... Yes! Yes! Campbell Reid, you are a genius!'

The rest of us glanced sideways at each other. In newspaperland the editor is always a genius. We just wished we knew what he was a genius for this time.

He whirled back around to survey our dumb blank faces.

'Oh for the love of God,' he said. 'Am I seriously stuck in here with the only three people in the universe who haven't read *The Da Vinci Code*?'

We all looked at our shoes mumbling. 'Er, no not yet ... Been meaning to but ... I've heard it's really good ...'

'Boys,' Campbell said, 'tomorrow we are going to sell a million newspapers.'

The next day the words 'DA VINCI CODE BLACKMAIL' blasted from the front page and my phone rang off the hook all morning – as I discovered hours later when I eventually woke up. Finally I was a real newspaper man. As for the sniper they never did catch him, but who cared? I had my first splash.

Truth and Reconciliation

A decade earlier, in the sweet careless fog of incinerated marijuana and teenage dreams that was Cardigan Street, an envelope had arrived in the post which Darrin had proudly presented to me, no doubt thinking this would count as good behaviour against his steadfast neglect of the dishes. Inside it was a cheque for fifty dollars and a note that read: 'Happy Birthday Ace. Love, G. and Joy'.

This was apparently a middle-class affectation he had picked up over the years in which our contact had gradually dwindled. I had seen Catherine's family members leave similar notes on the fridge addressed only to 'C' or 'D' or 'K', all scribbled out of casual love and familiarity. But *our* family never did that, not *my* family.

I was instantly gripped by the kind of wild fury that only teenage rage can generate. Not only had my father not known what present to get me, he hadn't even bothered to sign all the letters in his name. When my father called up to ask if the letter had arrived I told him I hated him and never wanted to speak to him again.

Of course it was not just the note or the fifty dollar cheque, which despite my impoverished state I tore in two.

It was the leaving when I was six and the failure to teach me how to kick a football or drive a car or all the things I needed to know to be a man. It was the refusal to go camping with me when I was ten because he and Joy were, as he said in the letter declining my request, an inseparable 'adult unit'. It was the refusal to visit my decadent and decrepit new home – which as a fellow hippie revolutionary I thought he would be so proud of – because Joy might react badly to the stale smoke.

'You don't have to bring her,' I'd said hopefully. 'You could come on your own.'

'I'm afraid that's not an option,' he'd replied.

* * *

Ten years later I'd calmed down. After a tear- and beer-infused stream of letters followed by some nervous phone calls I asked if we should meet. He replied that he and Joy would love that. After all, he was at pains to explain, it had been hard on her too.

Obviously my father was still a one-step-forward-two-steps-back kind of guy.

Still, my rage was long past, and like an adult to a child I softly but sternly told him that Joy wasn't part of the deal. Bewildered at these terms, he agreed.

My sister, however, refused to let me go into battle unarmed and insisted she come along as a kind of emotional chaperone. Even after the years of cheerful childhood beatings and miscellaneous torment I had inflicted upon her, as is the duty of all good older brothers, she had somehow emerged as my eternal protector.

'I'll be fine,' I protested, feeling in my bones this was something I must do alone.

'Oh bullshit, Joe,' my little sister said matter-of-factly. 'We both know you'll be a fucking wreck.'

It says something about my father's mental age that upon being told of my sister's presence he immediately sensed an ambush. 'Well if *you're* bringing someone how come *I* don't get to?' he demanded. I had to remind him both that we were his children and he wasn't a child anymore.

And so I flew back to Melbourne and the three of us walked and talked by the pelican-specked water around Williamstown Pier. My father looked thin and old, yet still wore a chin beard and a faded denim jacket that would have put most 65-year-old rock and rollers to shame. He was more nervous and small than I'd remembered from his towering days in my youth. Certainly shorter than Danny Bertossa and less wise than JC and with none of the supreme grandiosity of Bob Carr.

Amid enough small talk to fill a crowded restaurant, and my sister's diplomatically measured silences, I told him I had a girlfriend who I thought might just be the one and his ears pricked to attention.

'Is she a musician?' he asked hopefully.

'No,' I said.

'Oh,' he replied, and the conversation lulled again.

And so we turned the talk to politics, that great ender of silences.

'You know who I like as the next Labor leader?' he said. 'That guy Rudd.'

I caught my breath. I was a Latham man through and through and I had always presumed that however far apart my father and I had been in words and distance we would always end up thinking the same thoughts. Yet here we were, our divergent paths once more conjoined, and we'd landed in two completely different places. In his absence I had mown through a pantheon of heroes, from Danny Bertossa to Steve Harris to John Coomber to Bob Carr. Each of them had in one way or another taken me under their wing or made me feel special for one precious moment. My father hadn't even offered to pick me up from the airport.

As the sun settled down across Port Phillip Bay and the talk ran dry my father and sister and I silently nodded a conclusion to the evening. Annie drove us to the friend's place Greg and Joy were staying at and we got out to say our goodbyes. Maybe one of us knew we would never see each other again or maybe none of us did. Or maybe we all suspected it and didn't want to say. Either way I hugged him farewell and let my eyes absorb his greyed rectangular face, so happy, so confused, so distant and so much like mine.

'Come on,' my sister said as I got back in the car. 'Let's go home.'

'Yeah,' I said, and sat in silence for a while. Eventually, though, I couldn't keep it in any longer. 'Kevin Rudd!' I said. 'As if *he'll* ever be prime minister.'

A Fork in the Road

A few months after the meeting with my father, I was having a cigarette on the Holt Street roof with Penbo, who had gone from being the state political correspondent to chief of staff to opinion editor in less time than it took most people to take the elevator to the third floor. Naturally I idolised him enormously and so whenever we met I always made sure I had the poise and eloquence of a catatonic mule.

I was just in the middle of telling him how great he was when he abruptly changed the subject.

'Hey mate, do you want a column?' he asked.

I stood up straight as though someone had just stuck my hand in a toaster. 'Um, well, yeah,' I said. 'I'd love one.'

'Yeah right.' Penbo nodded his head with such intensity it looked like his chest was trying to attack his face.

He vaporised the last of his cigarette and lit up another in one seamless movement. It occurred to me that he was simply making a mental list of all the nagging narcissists who would be bugging him for page space that year.

'Er, why?' I said. 'I mean I don't want to put any noses out of joint.'

'Oh, don't worry about that,' he said.

'Honestly, I'm just happy where I am.'

'Yeah, well everybody thinks that.'

'Seriously though,' I said. 'You've got a full book. Whose spot could I even take?'

Penbo drew in another barrelful of smoke. 'I dunno,' he said. 'How about mine?'

The next day there was a rare silence in the newsroom as Campbell Reid gathered the troops around him and said he would be stepping down as editor for an executive job with News in Queensland. After pausing to allow for several muffled sobs from across the floor he announced that his replacement was one David Penberthy.

It is not easy to make a roomful of journalists gasp but that did the trick. Penbo was always destined for greatness but this was stratospheric even by his own standards. At 37 he was to be the youngest editor in *The Daily Telegraph*'s history. Virtually everyone wanted to see Penbo in the top job but no one wanted to see Campbell go.

Despite his young age Penbo had all the key requirements to be a *Telegraph* editor: a rare brilliance, a wicked sense of humour, a brutal work ethic, a love of beer and frequent flashes of madness. He had already displayed many of these qualities, not least during his groundbreaking Holden Eden-Monaro poll, in which he took a supercharged Holden Monaro to poll 600 people in Australia's infamous bellwether seat and thus correctly predicted the outcome of the 2004 federal election. However, now that he had adopted the mantle of leadership he needed someone else to perform such preposterous stunts on his behalf. As it turned out that august duty fell to me.

And so I soon found myself flying to Queensland to crash a Peter Beattie press conference with a six-foot square $636 million invoice for NSW's lost GST revenue, an act which did more than any other to warn the masses of the hitherto unknown horrors of horizontal fiscal imbalance. I also hit the 2007 campaign trail aboard a 1929 fire engine, a vehicle of questionable roadworthiness but unquestionable integrity which soon became known as 'The Truck of Truth'.

But Penbo's most inspired decision came when Kevin Rudd garrotted Kim Beazley with Julia Gillard's numbers and was crowned leader of the Australian Labor Party. Rudd immediately embarked upon a ten-day trip around the country, which he called a 'listening tour' of Australia. During the same speech he had also declared, approximately 28,000 times, that the nation was facing 'a fork in the road'. And so the *Telegraph* declared its own expedition, which we dubbed 'The Fork in the Road Tour'. And I was appointed its sole leader, sole organiser and, now that I think about it, sole member.

Rudd had already been flatfooted by the *Telegraph*, which had greeted his ascension with a front page picture of him staring at the camera with the headline: 'WHERE'S THE VISION KEVIN?' Having not even been in the job for 24 hours, Rudd felt this criticism of his leadership style was perhaps a tad premature.

However like virtually everything in politics and the media, the *Telegraph*'s approach to seismic political events is best understood through the prism of the 1996 alien invasion movie *Independence Day*, a film which contains enough real-life lessons to be classified as a documentary.

The discerning cinema-goer will recall the critical scene in which fighter ace and would-be space shuttle pilot Will Smith, having just downed a flying saucer, limps up to the spacecraft and opens the cockpit. Suddenly he is confronted by a hideous slimy monster with pointy teeth and menacing wavy tentacles. After being initially startled, Smith responds the only way he can think of and punches the little green fucker in the head.

This neatly sums up the *Telegraph*'s default position on new political leaders. We get presented with a completely foreign and untested entity that wants to take over and control our world; we don't know where it comes from, we don't know what it's capable of and we certainly don't know what it plans to do. And so we smack it in the face and see what happens.

Sometimes the alien responds by reconsidering its assessment of humans as a weak and easily dominated species and moderates any authoritarian instincts accordingly. Sometimes the alien responds by fighting back with a counter-argument as to why it truly does deserve to be in charge and delivers that plan accordingly. And sometimes the alien goes ballistic in a top-secret underground military facility and attempts to assassinate the President of the United States.

Now it was Rudd's turn. We'd challenged him to produce a cohesive and tangible vision and he'd responded that he bloody well would if we gave him half the chance. Being a fair and reasonable newspaper we offered to do just that. Penbo decided that I would follow Kevin Rudd every step of the way on the Fork in the Road Tour, and see just which particular prong he planned to poke the nation with.

Rudd the Great and Terrible

This wayward pilgrimage started with a community picnic in Rudd's suburban Brisbane electorate and then crisscrossed the entire country, covering every state, until it was due to wind up in Sydney. Over ten days I almost never left Rudd's side. At first it was me and the big-hitters from Canberra but they dropped off after 48 hours or so, grumbling about having real work to do, and were replaced by the gallery B-listers. Soon even they fell away after the caravan moved too far from the civility of the eastern seaboard. By the end I was the only journo to stay the course.

Then, as now, Rudd possessed a great vanity, an insatiable work ethic and a small-c Christian sense of duty, and the decision to follow the trail right to its bitter or otherwise end appealed to all three of these qualities. About halfway through Penbo and I had discussed pulling out – it was, after all, costing the paper a bomb to keep me going – but we both wanted to go the distance. Real politics didn't happen in the parliament or the press gallery, it happened out in the field, in the suburbs. And the true character of a leader wasn't tested at press conferences or during question time, it was when he was out in the real world and all the banal terror it contained.

It was always telling that while most journos and MPs were later quick to turn so viciously against Rudd, the broader public never did and those same journos and MPs always struggled to understand why. He was loved by the outsiders and hated by the insiders, a condition I couldn't help but feel an affinity with: Where he sat he couldn't belong and where he belonged he could never sit.

Either way the *Tele* wanted to uncover the man, uncoloured and unabridged, so that when he arrived in Sydney at the end of the tour, no doubt anticipating a Roman-style Triumph, we would be neither the marching lieutenants nor the waving masses but the humble slave standing behind him in the chariot whispering, 'Remember, you are mortal. Remember you are just a man ...'

Rudd and I hadn't known each other at all prior to that trip but by the end we knew each other well. There were already hints of the character flaws that are so amplified by positions of power – that brittle vanity being chief among them – but there was clearly something special about him. Unlike Kim Beazley, who is a naturally gregarious and engaging presence, Rudd has little instinctive warmth. Indeed, one sensed a kind of nervousness in social settings that he would try to cover up with self-aggrandising anecdotes and appalling dad jokes that he would then laugh at. At face value this could make him come across as a terrible narcissist but if you looked and listened with any depth you could easily perceive the insecurity it stemmed from. Having been an outcast at school myself I could spot another a mile away. It was hard to know how to be friendly to people when you'd never actually had any friends.

Yet despite this it was not uncommon for him to be literally mobbed by crowds wherever he went, even in those first days as Opposition Leader. There is no scientific explanation for why some politicians have this kind of magnetic attraction. Bob Hawke and Bill Clinton certainly possessed it, but for each of them it was the product of an almost messianic starpower. For Rudd it was more of an awkward nerdish charm that made people, young people in particular, go wild for him. At a cricket match at the WACA a crowd of young blokes was so desperate to get close to him that a group of them descended from the stands to virtually kidnap him and take him back to their spot. Thinking he was off-duty, Rudd had dismissed his advisers and I was the only one next to him.

'What do you think?' he asked hesitantly. 'Should I be worried?'

'I think you'd better do as they say,' I said.

In the end he was dragged like a football player who'd just kicked the winning goal up to an enclave of roaring blokes decked out in green and gold and with Australian flags plastered all over their skin. They enveloped him, cheering, and thrust beers underneath his chin, the only form of tribute they knew. There could not have been a better endorsement of nor advertisement for any Australian leader. A thousand politicians would kill for such a reception. Rudd, on the other hand, smiled nervously and pretended to sip at a cup of warm light beer – his lips hardly daring to touch the rim – while his eyes darted from side to side looking for an escape route.

This was Rudd's first real encounter with the mob and he could not have been more uncomfortable but he soon had no choice other than to get used to it. Several more times on the tour the response he got was more like a rock star than that of a politician, yet he was the most un-rock star politician one could imagine. Hawke would be all winks and smiles and back-claps and Clinton would be all that and more – hell, he even smoked pot and played the saxophone – but Rudd just grinned awkwardly with pursed lips and squinty eyes and nervously patted his hair. Yet the adulation just escalated and escalated until he confused himself for the god he almost was.

It was six months after the tour that Penbo called one evening while I was having drinks at the Gaslight Hotel in Surry Hills to both celebrate and commiserate my 31st birthday.

'Mate, I'm just on my way,' he said. 'Do you mind if I bring someone?'

About half an hour later Penbo appeared upstairs at the Gaslight, already looking a little discombobulated. The reason for this became clear when he shepherded through Kevin, who had struggled to make it through the door with his clothes intact. The Leader of Her Majesty's Opposition was instantly swamped by almost everyone in the room, overwhelmingly hipsters whose sole defining characteristic is cool indifference to anything adult, serious or mainstream. Kevin was nothing if not all of those things – indeed he had crafted his entire image around being all of those things – and yet kids were not just flocking to see him, they had even, in the midst of the commotion, formed an orderly queue.

Certainly neither Mark Latham nor Simon Crean nor even the eminently huggable Kim Beazley could have ever extracted such a response. The appeal of Hawke and Howard was far more mainstream and while Paul Keating could still cause oohs and aahs among Labor's true believers, his target demographic was, to say the least, boutique.

The Gaslight incident showed that Kevin, on the other hand, had achieved the impossible: For perhaps the first time in history an Australian politician had become cool.

Rudd's hubris was at least matched by an enormous intellect and he had a genuine and deeply held set of values that he always tried to marry to his ideas. He read widely and frequently examined his conscience. He may have been a cold political operator and even cold personally but his beliefs and the policies he put together to give them shape were warm. His sense of social justice was strong and genuine, even if he didn't behave justly to his own exhausted staff and colleagues. The critical mishandling of the *Oceanic Viking* debacle – in which Rudd was crippled by his Christian sense of duty to the asylum seekers and the political imperative that the government needed to show its force – was at least proof of his compassion towards human beings more wretched than overworked bureaucrats or slighted ministerial colleagues. Moreover his Apology to the Stolen Generation was his most human and genuine public moment, and the achievement he himself held most dear.

In other words Rudd's heart and his mind were in the right place, it was just the rest of him that tended to go AWOL. He was a leader who cared deeply about humanity, just not much about humans themselves.

Rudd the Campaigner

'The *what* theory?' Rudd blurted.

We were flying over Tasmania in a tiny charter plane and I noticed he was staring at the emergency exit and perhaps wondering where the parachutes were kept. It was early in the tour and clearly we were not as familiar with each other as I had thought.

Still, there was no turning back. 'Hogfucker' is one of those words that once said cannot really be unsaid.

'The Lyndon Johnson Hogfucker Theory. Don't tell me you haven't heard of it?'

'Er, no.' Now he was looking around for tape recorders.

'Okay, you know Lyndon Johnson right?'

'Jesus mate, I might not be Bob Carr but I'm not an idiot.'

'Okay, so the story goes that Lyndon Johnson was running for governor of Texas but the Republican guy was killing him. He was way behind in the polls – actually I dunno if they had polls back then but you know – and the election's around the corner and everyone just figures he's gone. So all his advisers go up to him and say: "What do we do Mr Johnson?" and LBJ sits back for a while and thinks.

Then he says: "The other guy – he's a hog farmer right?" And his advisers go: "Yeah, so what?" And he says: "I want you to get on the phones and start spreading a rumour that he fucks his hogs."'

Rudd raised his eyebrows and ratcheted back his seat a notch.

'So suddenly his staff are horrified, and they say, "But boss! We can't say that. We're never going to be able to prove it." And LBJ just looks at them like they're idiots ...'

'So what does he say?' Rudd asked.

'That's the best bit,' I said. 'He says: "I don't want you to *prove* it. I just want to hear him *deny* it."'

Rudd snorted and shifted uncomfortably in his chair. 'Right, I'll remember that,' he said, and rearranged the pages of his newspaper to signal the end of the conversation.

I sat there feeling somewhat out of place but, being trapped in a small aircraft 10,000 feet somewhere above Launceston, my options of removing myself were, like Kevin's, somewhat limited. Then after a few awkward minutes there was a conspicuous rustling in Rudd's lap.

'Hm,' he said.

I looked over and saw his back return to the upright position. He leaned towards me and thrust the newspaper onto my lap. In the middle of the page was an op-ed by John Howard defending his Work Choices policy against the chorus of attacks from unions and the Labor Party. The headline read: 'I AM NOT AN EXTREMIST: HOWARD'. Rudd tapped it with a thick well-manicured finger.

'Hogfucker theory?'

I nodded.

'So what ended up happening to Lyndon Johnson in that race?' he asked.

'He won,' I said, but in fact I had no idea. It was just a story my father had told me and you don't know if some stories are true until you tell them.

* * *

After that conversation Rudd and I chatted more and more frequently and more and more freely, but when it came to the business of newsmaking – well, business was business. During every one of the daily press conferences on the tour I would ask not a single question – lest any of the other journos find out what I was chasing – then after it was over I would buttonhole him either on the footpath or on the plane or in the back seat of a car or anywhere I could pin him down and try to extract what information I could.

And so if we'd been to a school I'd demand to know what he was going to do in education. If we'd been to a factory I'd demand to know what he was going to do in industrial relations. If we'd been to a hospital I'd demand to know what he was going to do about health funding. Sure, maybe I liked the guy, but that didn't mean I couldn't be an arsehole about it.

Naturally he and his staff would try to say that no set decisions had been made, at which point I would pull out my handy pocketbook of all Mark Latham's policies of 2004 and ask which ones he was going to scrap.

'Oh, so this is now in doubt is it? You're axing teddy bears for children with cancer?'

'Hang on a minute,' a weary Rudd would sigh and quickly huddle with his advisers. 'Alright. No, we're not axing teddy bears for children with cancer. You can quote me on that.'

And so another story was born. I sometimes wonder if it was my incessant brow-beating in his first days as Opposition Leader that led Kevin into his ultimate death spiral of policy on the run. No doubt there were many more than me but every time he got crucified for it I couldn't help but feel a trickle of blood on the wrists.

Either way, soon the gallery journos were complaining to Rudd that he was giving stories to me instead of them. Even the *Tele*'s own Canberra bureau was complaining to Penbo that they should have been the ones getting the scoops. Generously, Rudd's and Penbo's responses were the same: If they wanted the stories maybe they should have been on the road chasing them instead of sitting in an office waiting for them to fall through the air-conditioning duct.

During one pitstop in the middle of the tour Rudd visited a dental clinic in suburban Melbourne and this triggered in me a tsunami of traumatic childhood memories. Afterwards I bailed him up in my usual fashion but this time it was me who had a story for him.

I proceeded to recount to the new leader my tale of orthodontic woe and my ultimate gratitude to the national dental health scheme for giving me the privilege of being able to smile in public. But it ought not be a privilege, I said. Everyone should have the right to smile without fear of other people gasping. How many jobs had been lost, romances cruelled or other life disappointments endured because someone was too poor or unlucky to have a decent set of teeth? Now the federal scheme that gave so many pensioners and children of pensioners both the ability and the reason to smile had been axed by the Howard government. It was a shame, I said, a deep shame. Good teeth were the emblem of a good society.

Rudd nodded his head in the non-committal way that all politicians master.

'So what do you suppose we should do about it?'

'Well,' I said, 'as it turns out I have the old Labor policy right here ...'

Rudd narrowed his eyes and gave a half smile.

'Hm,' he said. 'Call me later.'

The next day we broke the story that a newly elected Labor government would introduce a nationwide dental health scheme with a focus on patients from lower socio-economic backgrounds. Rudd later formed a National Health and Hospitals Reform Commission which eventually declared a Medicare-style dental scheme a matter of national priority. Two years after that first conversation, the phone rang as I was frantically bumbling out of my tiny Darlinghurst flat and straggling down the road trying to button up my shirt.

'Hello?' I puffed.

'I just wanted to let you know that we've done it,' said the Prime Minister.

After the usual delays and political infighting and policy wranglings my tale of a poor boy's orthodontic woe eventually became the $4 billion dental scheme announced by Julia Gillard and Tanya Plibersek in 2012. It says something about the bottlenecks and chaos Rudd created that it was his hated successor who finally cut the ribbon on the scheme more than five years after it was first conceived. But it also says something about Rudd's integrity that he started it at all and that he called to give a lowly reporter a small amount of undue credit. If he really was a cunt, then he seemed like a pretty decent cunt to me.

Purgatory

Another year or two later after an unremarkable day at the office, a couple of kindly colleagues spirited me over the road to toast in my 34th birthday. We were sitting amid the utilitarian concrete and steel of the Aurora Hotel, which was basically an extension of the *Telegraph* newsroom in those headier days, when the phones started ringing.

My good friend Tim Blair, perhaps the world's most lovable right-wing columnist, was sitting opposite me.

'I'm telling you man, it's happening,' he said.

'They're reporting it on the ABC,' said a sub who'd just sat down uninvited.

'There you go,' said Tim. 'Even the subs know.'

'Since when have you ever believed anything on the ABC?' I said. 'You think the whole organisation is a government conspiracy.'

'You want a government conspiracy?' said Tim, a smile breaking over his face like a wave. 'There's one happening right now and it's happening against *your mate*.'

'He's not my mate,' I protested emptily. 'He's a first-term fucking prime minister and no party would be stupid enough to roll a first-term prime minister.'

'Oh, I can think of one that might be,' Tim said, and gulped a celebratory dose of cheap chardonnay.

Then Tim's mobile phone rang, which stunned me into silence. Blair kept his mobile number hidden from everyone. As far as I knew I was his best friend and he hadn't even given it to me.

'Yep,' he told the receiver and then hung up. 'Well,' he said cheerfully, 'I'd best be getting back to the office.'

Tim grabbed the empty laptop bag he always carried around with him for reasons still unknown and strode out humming a tune I could've sworn was 'The Internationale'. If it was the intention of the ALP caucus to give right-wingers shivers of delight then they had achieved their goal impeccably.

'Fuck,' I said to nobody. 'I am never going to forgive them for this.'

Word had been circulating for months about Gillard planning to roll Rudd — naturally first broken by the *Telegraph* — and then on the morning of the coup the *Sydney Morning Herald* ran a story about Gillard being so outraged that Rudd suspected she was planning to knife him she decided she had no choice but to do as he'd predicted. Even more incredibly the caucus and the Canberra press gallery seemed to see this as a perfectly rational argument. Jesus, I thought. Am I completely alone?

Certainly in the literal sense that appeared to be the case. Within seconds every journo had vacated the pub to rewrite the second edition and I was sitting there swearing at the smoky air, which never answered back. As the clock ticked over to midnight I entered my 35th year, angry and abandoned once more.

The Long Walk Home

On the exact same day 23 years before I was sitting huddled with my sister and cousins in a darkened bedroom just after midnight.

'Should we really do it?' one cousin asked.

'Yeah,' I said. 'It's gonna be alright.'

In that small dark room of thick timber and woollen blankets we were as safe and protected as any kids could be. After some frantic rustling we broke out blocks of chocolate, large noisy bags of chips and other plastic packets of sticky lollies that could cause parents to wake. Little did we know this was the slightest of our worries. No parent in the house had slept in days.

The place was Wilsons Promontory, a wild and ill-earthed land at the bottom of the Australian continent. With rare largesse the family had forsaken the usual tent arrangements and set up in some modest wooden huts near the tourist settlement of Tidal River. It was, I suppose, as likely a place as any for the impossible to happen.

My mother of course could not tolerate a day without physical exercise or some other form of intense communion with the natural world. And so on our first day the whole family was rounded up and taken for a bushwalk along the Lilly Pilly track.

Paddy loved nothing more than bushwalking. A bushwalk was, after all, wandering without end, a path going ever forward. He was a kid who liked to stick to the road. The forest on either side was calming and the way ahead was clear. In the city he could dart off in any number of directions but in the bush he never left the track. And so my mother would take him, and thus all of us, on frequent bushwalks through every national park within driving distance of our home. It always thrilled Paddy, even if the rest of us were less impressed by the same bunch of trees rotating around us.

This was a well-trodden track barely four kilometres in length and as wide as a road. Tour buses would stop off in the carpark to let elderly Japanese couples hobble through its gently gradated circuit on zimmer frames. This was no Everest. It was a mild, gravel-strewn, heavily travelled path with toilets and picnic areas and signposts every step of the way. You could have driven a fucking bus through it.

And so we all strolled lazily along the path spread out like a phalanx, with a couple of kids straggling behind and Paddy a few short metres ahead. Then he rounded a bend and we never saw him again.

* * *

We all, at one point or another in our lives, wonder with rage and regret where things went so wrong. We all try to find the point in time when we could have changed our sorry destinies and set the course for a different path if only we could reach back. As we turned the corner amid the rich southern tree ferns and mountain ash and saw the path empty ahead of us our whole lives became instantly forlorn. In a single tick of the clock we were all broken.

At first, of course, there was hope. Paddy could not have wandered far and a few shouts would no doubt bring him running back again as they always had. Then when they didn't the rangers were called. But as night settled in they had still found no trace of him.

Over the next hours and then days the search escalated until it became the biggest manhunt in Victorian history. It led all the TV news bulletins and Wilsons Prom was soon swarming with cops, SES volunteers and journalists all desperately trying to find the 'Little Boy Lost'. Meanwhile my mother descended into a state of anxiety and sorrow it is beyond my powers to describe.

Despite the noblest and most exhaustive efforts my brother was never found. The only thing recovered was a plastic yellow rain hat that he loved beyond reason. He called it his fireman's hat and it was an object he would never have let go of willingly.

While the adults dealt with their wrenching guts, we children discussed what should be done about the midnight feast for which we had so long prepared. It might have been easy to suggest the pithy line 'It's what he would have wanted' but this was unthinkable to us given we had no doubt he would at any moment be walking through the door. Instead we celebrated the news that the police search and rescue squad were calling in their new hi-tech helicopters to scan the bushland for signs of life with heat-detecting infra-red cameras. Any excuse to eat the chocolate. Any excuse to believe that the world would always right itself. There was, after all, no problem on Earth that grown-ups couldn't solve.

'It's gonna be alright,' I assured the group. 'They've got the heat-seekers out now.'

The younger kids nodded in agreement and we all tore into the rich crinkly packages of sweets.

The only one to abstain was my older cousin Karina who instead cried quietly into the bunched up blankets on the floor. I offered her a jelly snake and told her everything would be fine.

* * *

The following day the kids were bundled together and told we had to go back to Melbourne. The heat-seekers had found no warm glow to light up the freezing forest. My father, who had arrived on the scene with Joy but declined to join the search party on the grounds that 'they know what they're doing', was instructed to courier the children away from the trauma that the adults were now bracing themselves to face.

Ever wary of responsibility, my father protested that there wasn't enough room in his VW Kombi and, when the laws of physics proved otherwise, said he didn't have enough seatbelts — a somewhat misplaced concern for childhood safety given the circumstances.

With my mother at her ragged end, my uncle Johnny, a soul so gentle he made Gandhi look like Saddam Hussein, quietly stepped forward and put his face close against my father's so as to speak all the more softly to him.

'Greg,' he whispered, 'I don't care about the fucking seatbelts. You will take these children home.'

That night, on the long straight road out of Wilsons Prom, I stared out the window into the dark still shapes of the bushland that seemed to be exorcising us like a demon. Somewhere in there my brother's body lay but I knew we would never find him. The blackness told me so, as did my mother's broken eyes.

Atop the shuddering engine of the old German motor beneath the front passenger seat, my father's finely tuned musician's ears picked out my heaving sobs in the back. He told Joy to pull the van over, leaned across and dragged me into the seat next to him with his wide hands.

'Okay,' he said. 'Drive.'

I sat there with my father's long arm around me and cried into his navy blue parka which rustled and undulated at a slow steady beat. After a while I figured out he was crying too and so with nothing that could be said and no place else to go we both kept crying until the lights of the city came blurring into our eyes.

Arrival

Inevitably we all want to go back from whence we came, and I can still remember that first gulp of Melbourne oxygen every time I stepped outside the glass doors at Tullamarine. The sparser, crisper air that made both the high sky and the needling rain all the more empty and fresh. My mother's junk-filled red Nissan hatchback puttering up to the wrong designated collection point, her manic smile carving through mouldy towels, foam rubber kickboards and tattered children's books as she struggled with the dicky door lock to let me in.

This was home. The life I'd left too soon at seventeen to chance my luck in the big city, and the one I left again six years later for a bigger city wrapped around a harbour and a dream.

A few days later we'd be back in the same place at the same airport and as the door creaked open with the sound of grinding rusted metal that same air would rush in as I stepped out. And every time it would create the same cyclonic swirl of memory: Her heroic rescuing of me from lonely schoolyard torment, her painstaking efforts to dress me as a gaylord Superman just as I'd wanted, her hurt bafflement as to why I kept running away from home, and her efforts to keep me there by constantly making me any food I wanted, her doling out of her precious few fifty dollar bills and innumerable homemade pizzas when she drove me back to my share-house hovels, her desperate attempts to clean up the house before Catherine arrived, her endless unconditional offers of anything, anything, anything, and my constant desire for something more.

All of those memories would explode at once each time I got out of the car and made my backward pilgrimage towards the terminal. And every time I said the same thing.

'Bye Mum.'

Then the cabin doors close and 90 minutes later you're 800 kilometres and a world away banking over the Harbour Bridge. I have never really understood how that happens.

* * *

There are two ways of flying into Sydney: with tears and without. Every refugee in that glittering city of immigrants is running from something or running towards it. Sydney is a siren; either you stay on the boat and try to block your ears to its call or you jump in the water and start swimming for your life.

Soon, of course, the jumper regrets his decision and can't tell the difference between the saltwater all around him and that which is streaming from his eyes. You wonder why you're in this place, with sharks always encircling and jagged rocks on every shore.

Sydney is a city made for television, a city made for pretty pictures and bright colours and movement and loudness. It's like it was discovered two centuries early just waiting for the First Fleet re-enactment to come along.

Thus it was that after years of desperation in more than one Sydney flat and more than one Sydney news outlet, a variety of people who should have known better started suggesting I should go on television.

My real foray began when I was invited to appear on Sky News to commentate on the 2007 NSW election debate, which fortunately nobody had watched. My first words were: 'I- I- I- th … think th- th- th- Opposition Leader was rath- th- th- ther awkward.' It was, as my erstwhile spin doctor friend Peter Lewis put it, a somewhat ironic opening statement.

However I soon discovered that incompetence was no impediment to entry in the televisual arts. When you write you have to think, you have to pore over facts, dig up numbers and names from distant corners of the brain. You have to pause and reflect and wonder. Worst of all you have to remember. And you have to do all of it alone.

But in the magical world of television you don't have to think. Instead you just have to *say* what you think and say it louder than everybody else and at the end of it you get a bunch of people telling you how great you are. If people hate you in TV land they at least have the decency to say it behind your back.

At last I realised I didn't have to be deep and brooding and intelligent anymore. I could just be happy and stupid. It was like a tangled grey cloud had unravelled from my head. Soon I was being happy and stupid on just about every television and radio station in the country. If that was what it took to make it in Sydney then it was good enough for me.

Yet even the lights and delights of television couldn't explain the first time I'd got that strange and certain feeling. It didn't explain the time that I'd left my smiling watery-eyed mother at Melbourne Airport once more, just a day or so after I'd left my puzzled and forlorn father on a garden path somewhere in the suburbs around Williamstown. How many parents could one abandon in 48 hours I wondered.

I was flying into Sydney with the inverted crooked teeth of the Opera House smiling up at me and the water so deep and blue you could scarcely see the sharks beneath. The usual jagged tear in my chest started to heal as soon as I'd buckled up my seatbelt but by the time the CBD skyscrapers loomed into view, clutched together like pieces of straw in a fist, I felt another sensation I had never experienced before. I rummaged up and down between my turning stomach and burning throat trying to divine its origin or its purpose. My head was light and my breath was accelerating and I wondered if I was airsick or hungover sick or just having a heart attack. But then I realised it was something far more profound and frightening than that.

It was the feeling of coming home.

Acknowledgements

A book of this nature is essentially and inevitably a horribly narcissistic exercise. It involves delving into levels of introspection and self-exposition that would make even the most hardened psychopath blush with shame. As a result it has been a somewhat lonely journey yet at the same time impossible to divorce from all those who kept me alive and functional enough to produce such a work.

Those mentioned in these pages will know their worth, although many more have been stripped of their legacy or defamation during the long hard editing process. Among them are a couple of ex-girlfriends who had a profound effect on me but whose lessons failed to meet the exacting requirement of the narrative arc. To them I say thank you and, for reasons we both understand, I am deeply sorry.

There are also many friends who, whether they knew it or not, made the difference between me staying in Sydney and coming to the point where I was able to write this story and going home to Melbourne in what Alan Jones might describe as a chaff bag. I owe them an unspeakable debt of gratitude.

Speaking of Melbourne, there is an enormous chapter of this book – or better yet the whole contents of another

– as yet unwritten about my great friend Matt Lennox, whose early exploits are detailed herein. His borderline superhuman partner, Estelle, deserves to be mentioned if only for the small fact that she has kept him and my two godsons happy and safe on this planet. I remain distressed by the fact they are living in sin.

Sydneyside, I could not go without mentioning my most dysfunctional best friend Byron, whose ongoing litany of crises sustains me, nor our frequent comrade in arms Goz, who is as deeply strange as he is deeply beloved.

There are also many colleagues and mentors who are no less friends and whose presence in this book is truncated or denied only for reasons of length or narrative flow. Some, as editors, would appreciate this. John Coomber and my great champion at the *Telegraph*, Penbo, are worth mentioning again. Without them there is no doubt I would never have come to a position where I was able to write these words. I would also be remiss and somewhat suicidal if I did not thank my resurrector, Boris, who gave me a new lease of life at the *Telegraph* and is the hardest newsman I have ever met. In all my time in journalism I have never been so infuriated by nor learned so much from a single man. The great mandarin of Australian television Peter Meakin is also someone to whom I owe a mighty debt for his wise counsel and a level of support that was as unexpected as it was unyielding. They all call me mate but the truth is they are like fathers to me.

Likewise I must thank Jeni O'Dowd for her incredible support, invaluable tutelage and red-hot inside information.

A special acknowledgement must also go to my very good friend Timmy G, who despite having played no role whatsoever in the composition of this book, nor having displayed even the slightest intention of reading it, nonetheless has insisted on being given a mention.

But more than any of the above my ultimate gratitude goes to the distinctly unmusical girl my father once so casually disapproved of. Her name is Tara, and without her it is not just this book that would be unwritten but also the life of the man who wrote it.

It is thanks to her that I am able to function and, more importantly, it is thanks to her that I am able to bring a new being into this ridiculous world. And so, lastly, I give her my thanks, my love, and my life.

www.ingramcontent.com/pod-product-compliance
Lightning Source LLC
Chambersburg PA
CBHW022036290426
44109CB00014B/869